~ PRAISE FOR ~
"THE JACKRABBIT FACTOR"

"This book compellingly shows the power of goal setting, starting with gratitude. It affirms the reader's proactive capacities in exercising the initiative in improving one's life. Its powerful lessons are based on a fascinating and inspiring story, which, in a simple way, empowers the reader potentially to also do extraordinary things. Leslie lives what I teach." ~ **Dr. Stephen R. Covey, author, The 7 Habits of Highly Effective People and The 8th Habit: From Effectiveness to Greatness**

"I have seldom read a more impactful book where true principles are taught in such a clear and simple analogy. I have spent many years teaching people how to gain control of their time and ultimately their lives. The principles so uniquely taught in "The Jackrabbit Factor" take everything I have done a step further. How so you say? You will have to read it to find out. This is a book that must be experienced and not described. The person who can comprehend and internalize the laws of thought as they are beautifully analogized in these pages, will realize any dream, effect any change, achieve any goal they desire. A must read." ~ **Hyrum W. Smith, Co-founder Franklin Covey, CEO Galileo**

"I am genuinely impressed. Leslie has created a jewel in 'The Jackrabbit Factor.' It has been crafted such that a person can read and re-read it, and each time glean something new and empowering. In a unique and creative way, Leslie's story will lead her readers through

successively increased levels of awareness and leave them not only with an uncommon confidence, but more importantly, with the ability to make any life change they desire. Success-seekers of all degrees of knowledge and experience will benefit from this remarkable story. I strongly recommend you purchase multiple copies of this book for your family and friends." **~ Bob Proctor, founder Life Success Productions and best selling author of "You Were Born Rich"**

"I am actually at a loss for words after reading your manuscript. Kind of almost shook a little bit if that makes sense...The book was so well put together from a literary standpoint and the storyline was fantastic. It encompassed all the books that I have read so far and rolled it up into one. Though new at this for 9 months now, I have read close to 45 to 50 books/seminars from Jim Rohn, Bob Proctor, Brian Tracy, Randy Gage, Anthony Robbins, Lisa Jimenez, Cynthia Kersey, Tina Shearon and Carol Gates. You somehow rolled all those principles of the aforementioned people and placed it into one book. Of course I could see Wallace D Wattles throughout as well...It was a privilege to be able to read your manuscript." **~ Fred Schofield, independent IT consultant**

"This outstanding allegory is masterfully told in a clear, easy to understand manner. It is a comprehensive look at how we co-create our lives and determine our results through the power of thought. Leslie has woven every important life principle and universal law into this inspirational little book. I couldn't put it down! The

Jackrabbit Factor is destined to be not only an international bestseller, but a classic, and should be part of everyone's success library. I know it will become required reading for all my coaching clients! Thank you Leslie." **~ Camille Kocsis, President Successful Living Seminars, Master Success Coach, Speaker and Author**

"For 15 years I have helped people achieve financial freedom in Real Estate and the Stock Market, but I have discovered that those who actually make it happen have first experienced a significant switch in their mentality and attitude. I am convinced that this unassuming, but powerful story will actually facilitate that shift for those who are finally ready to live the abundant life, no matter what their vehicle to freedom may be. Furthermore, if they don't know their vehicle, this will teach them how to find the right vehicle and road map." **~ Mark Larson, two time best selling author of Trade Stocks Online and Technical charting for Profits**

"[This story is] amazing! I'm near tears, on page [undisclosed]. This is hitting home. You have no idea how much I needed this, right this moment. Wow. Thank you. I'm writing down all that I know I will have. I have much to do, starting with being thankful to God for all my blessings." (Later...) "Okay, I'm in tears now! And feeling better and more positive, loved, guided and directed than I ever have in my entire life. I can't even begin to tell you how bad this day started, or the day before, but I know how it's going to end! Thank you so

much for sharing [this story] with me. You are amazing! Just amazing. And you know what? So am I!"
~ Suzanne Staten, single mother

"Leslie has a winner here! From the first words you are gripped immediately by the story. Cancel your plans for the next day and spend it with The Jackrabbit Factor."
~ Korby Waters, President, Breakthrough Academy, LLC

"WOW! I just finished reading "The Jackrabbit Factor." I moved so quickly through the story that by the end, I felt like I had been talking to a friend for a few hours, instead of reading. You are truly a master story-teller, and I just couldn't put the book down. You've brilliantly woven in all the secrets I've ever learned about how to tap into the extraordinary power of your mind to be, do, or have anything you want. "The Jackrabbit Factor" lays out in narrative form a simple yet powerfully effective blueprint that virtually anyone can follow in order to consciously create their own circumstances and transform their lives." **~ Dimitri Mastrocola, retired attorney, success coach, founder www.SuccessCounsel.com**

"I'm thoroughly impressed and inspired. In the same tradition as 'Richest Man in Babylon' and 'Who Moved My Cheese,' 'The Jackrabbit Factor' dives much deeper into how the mind works and how good things are attracted into our lives without all the competition. I've studied a number of motivational/self-help books and programs to somehow figure out how to accomplish my

PRAISE FOR "THE JACKRABBIT FACTOR"

*goals. This book was insightful because it helped me realize that it is truly about **my** dream and what motivates **me**. I can relax and know that as I cultivate my desires properly, all that I want is on its way; in fact, it is already here."* ~ **Jeff Ackley, salesman, husband and father of five**

"Well, I must say I'm amazed. You certainly have a knack for this. I guess I need to go write my goals down!" ~ **Marcie Bringhurst, owner of www.windmill-designs.com and mother of six**

"In the form of a charming allegory, Householder sets out the steps necessary to identifying and achieving goals. It's a heartwarming story, easy to identify with. Not only did I read this book, I actually put its precepts into practice. I am happy to report that it works! Several times daily I find myself visualizing that fistful of jackrabbits, which reminds me to focus so keenly on my goal that I can actually see it, feel it, smell it, and hear it. If it can work for me, it can work for you, too. I heartily recommend THE JACKRABBIT FACTOR, and wish you all success as you realize your goals in life." ~ **Marcia Schutte, www.HeartlandReviews.com**

"This powerful modern day fable is a must for anyone who is sincerely interested in achieving success. If you're the type that persists but still gets nowhere, you MUST read this book today!" ~ **Zev Saftlas, founder www.EmpoweringMessages.com**

v

"I was so happy to read your work with my family... I learned with them and in the process, knew that I was reading something inspiring. As I walked with Richard through the pages, I felt good knowing that wealthy, wise mentors do exist and want to share. I think that as a young adult I would have put this book up there with Jonathan Livingston Seagull--SOAR HIGH, BE AWARE, AND LIVE!" ~ **Carolyn Tahauri, wife and mother of six**

"I have finished The Jackrabbit Factor and I am in awe...Leslie is so bright, so talented and an excellent writer. The trail she so cleverly wove through this story masterfully eliminated the, "yes, but" until I quit saying it, and then I stopped thinking it. I like her question when she refers to other programs which...add a clarifier "results not typical": Then she asks: "But why are the results not typical"? That's when I have doubts about any process but God's. She is masterful with applying this to all people and all situations. I like very much that she is the result of being schooled herself in the process and testifies it works for her. She covers all of the rationalizations one by one and leaves you with a willingness to try. She covers the inevitable slipping back into old patterns and sweetly exposes all of our attitudes. I appreciate the wiping out of competition and eliminating fear. It exposes society and strips away pride...and then comes gratitude. She is amazing with her words, what a great title for a lesson or program." ~ **Carole Reid Burr, co-author of Rose Marie Reid, An Extraordinary Life Story**

PRAISE FOR "THE JACKRABBIT FACTOR"

"Some books are about issues; some are about people. I perceive that "The Jackrabbit Factor" is about feelings. It is the kind of book you'll want to share with those with whom you have a caring relationship. Because it is such an easy "read," you will turn the last page and wish there was more". **- Dave Yoho, Author, "Have A Great Year Every Year," www.HaveAGreatYear.com**

"I just devoured your book...I am sitting here in tears because you cannot understand what a blessing and inspiration you have been to me in my life and how I would like to let you know that it is a privilege to say that I know you! I am crying because I was really moved by the story of Richard and his family and you don't know how many times I have asked the same questions that Richard asks himself in the beginning of the story and tried to lever myself out of the hole that I have been in. I have always believed that positive thought and faith have helped me to stay strong and persevere but after reading your book I realize that maybe it is time that I can do more than just get by." **~ Wendy Valentine, mother of three**

"[I just] finished reading the book - FANTASTIC. You made it so simple by explaining it through a story rather than an instructional guide. I have never read anything like it." **~ John Priest**

"The Jackrabbit Factor makes it all so simple. Unlike advice that is often easier said than done, this story illustrates that it really can be easy! Abundance, joy, and contentment are already within our grasp. There is

freedom in realizing the power our thoughts have to create both the good and the bad in our lives, and that is what this simple, straightforward story so clearly illustrates." **~Jon Portillo, Financial Advisor**

"Never has learning something this profound been so captivating. You won't want to put it down until you find out how the problem is resolved... and THEN it really cranks your gears! I'll never be the same."
~ Marnie Pehrson, founder
www.BelieversAtWork.com

And finally, I couldn't resist including what my very own father had to say. It certainly put a smile on *my* face:

"Leslie, I read your Jackrabbit Factor on the plane down today. Wow, I am totally impressed and quite embarrassed about my approach to all I do. Hey, all I gotta do is take LesterLessons and away we go! What I had read before was only a precursor to what you've created now, and the testimonials... will you remember me when you are on Oprah and raking in the big bucks? Just a few crumbs from your table.... I'm bursting with pride (is that bad?), think I'll just stand up and shout I KNOW LESLIE HOUSEHOLDER in my conference sessions this week. They might take me away, ha ha, but who cares! Give all them kinder a hug for me; sorry the conference isn't in Phoenix, maybe next year. Love, Pops"

"You will be able to move forward with confidence in pursuit of your dreams. You'll know who to listen to, and you'll be able to trust what they say. In short, you will be able to proceed methodically toward your worthy ideal, whatever it may be."

~*Leslie Householder, "The Jackrabbit Factor"*

THE
JACKRABBIT
FACTOR

Why You Can

THE
JACKRABBIT
FACTOR

Why You Can

Leslie Householder

THOUGHTSALIVE BOOKS

ThoughtsAlive Books
PO Box 31749
Mesa, AZ 85275

Third Edition February 2007
(Second Edition May 2006, First Edition August 2005)
Printed in the U.S.A.

ISBN 0-9765310-1-1
Library of Congress Catalog Card Number: 2005903973

Dedicated to...

all who, like me, have wanted to give up on their
dreams, but decided to take just one more step...

and

John W. Sims, because so many of my personal
victories are based upon the principles I learned
through just a handful of his stories
many years ago.

~ ACKNOWLEDGEMENTS ~

While this book is based on one of John W. Sims's brief analogies, I've had many a mentor along the way. My thanks go to each one of them:

John W. and Barbara Sims, who instilled within my husband and me a desire to never stop thinking, learning, and growing, no matter what we decided to do with our lives.

Steve, Denise, and the entire Pierce family for the countless hours they all invested in helping us to succeed. We're grateful for the many conversations; each of which created almost imperceptible, but significant shifts in our thinking. We hope they're each blessed beyond measure for all they did unselfishly for so long.

Aaron Tilton, for the casual conversation in the grocery store which eventually led to our introduction to the Pierce family.

Dr. Stephen R. Covey, (though we've never met) for graciously discarding the bookmark with Einstein's picture on it that read, "I want to know God's thoughts, the rest are details." At a time during my starving student days, I was the cleaning lady who swiped it from his trash and treasured its message. I believe I've since discovered just a few of those "thoughts."

Bob Proctor, for solidifying many morsels of wisdom we had tried to comprehend before, and helping us use the 'stickman concept' to finally launch our rocket.

Marnie Pehrson, author of "Lord, Are You Sure?" and founder of www.IdeaMarketers.com, for the abundant encouragement and generous web-related work, helping me take my message to the online world.

Kathryn Palmer, for her longtime friendship and knowledgeable editorial help.

Bob Spears, for his dedicated assistance in the final editing stages and for his amazing willingness to help on a moment's notice while recuperating from a total knee replacement. I was fortunate to discover his services at www.HeartlandReviews.com.

My gratitude goes out to Steve Nissle of Nissle Photography (www.nisslephoto.com) for doing such a fantastic job on the 'author's photo,' and for the ever patient Tim King of Click Graphics (www.clickgraphicsonline.com) for creating such a striking and meaningful cover design (and for putting up so well with one very fickle client).

Jana Stanfield, for composing the song, "If I Were Brave" which has moved me time and again to keep on pursuing my dreams. If she only knew how often its message has fueled me on through the rough times!

Thanks especially to my good parents, Bob and Carol Robertson who raised me to have faith, and think deeply; and who prepared me well for a life of learning out of the best books. I am grateful for all of the rapid feedback and suggestions on this project. I'm even glad my mother was honest with me about certain parts that just *had* to go, like the part when...oh, never mind... (Okay, Mom, you can stop laughing now...)

Also, thanks to the hundreds of others who said or did just the right thing at the right time as they crossed our path. Some are professional speakers and motivators, and some are just remarkable individuals who have walked with us along the way. We'd like to express our thanks for the mentorship of those ordinary people who are doing such extraordinary things. Certainly all of you have no idea what you have done for us. We cannot measure how much each one of you have influenced our lives for the better.

Many, many thanks to my friends who came on board to help me with my book launch: Adam Eason, Angelo M., Ann Stewart, Barbara Clements, Bernadette Doyle, Dr. Brad Swift, Camille Kocsis, Carien Theunissen, Cathy Stucker, Charlotte Burton, Chris Read, Christine Donnolo, Dale Kurow, David DeFord, Dawn Fields, Dimitri Mastrocola, Don Nicholes, Eric V. Van Der Hope, Eva Gregory, Father Dave, Fernando Soave, Glenna Burdick, Gracina Fulcher, Helen Halton, Ingela Berger, Irena Whitfield, Jan Wallen, Javed

Akram, Jeanette Cates, Jeffrey Tahauri, Jennifer Stewart, Jim Namaste, Joan Schramm, Joyce Pierce, Julian Kalmar, Karen Timothy, Katharine Hansen, Kathryn Martyn, Kathy Schneider, Keith Thirgood, Ken Burnett, Kevin Eikenberry, Kimberly Chastain, Lisa Preston, Liz Sumner, Lorraine Cohen, Lyn Cikara, Marc Gamble, Marnie Pehrson, Nelson Tan, Nicole Whitney, Pamela Geiss, Paul and Layne Cutright, Randall Stafford, Randy Gilbert, Rick Beneteau, Robert Wilkens, Robin Tramble, Sam Pennywell, Sheri Rowland, Sonny Julius, Terri Zwierzynski, Tim Ong, Tony Farrell, Tony Rathstone, Viveca Stone, Vivi Gonzales, Wendy Y. Bailey, Wendy McClelland, Wes Hopper, Whitney Ransom, Zev Saftlas, and the others who came on board, even after it was too late to mention their name here. It's been a genuine pleasure. Success to each of you!

A *huge* thanks to my six beautiful children for their patience and help as I prepared this book, letting me have "my turn" at my computer so often. They were so helpful in keeping the family running when I was "in the zone."

And finally, to my husband for his enduring, unconditional love and support. I'd like to say to him, "This has been an exhilarating journey; I am grateful to share so many common goals with you, and I expect to keep 'reaching for the stars' with you forever. You're my best friend."

~ TABLE OF CONTENTS ~

THE
JACKRABBIT
FACTOR

~ PREFACE ~

John W. Sims, a highly successful businessman, spoke of a time when he was traveling with an associate. The associate said, "John, aren't you going to put on your seatbelt?"

John replied with his raspy tenor voice, "Why, are we going to get into a crash?"

"Well, no, but you know, seatbelts save lives...,"

John retorted abruptly in his usual blunt way, "Seatbelts don't save lives."

"Of course they do! See, I was driving down the road with my family and something told me to make sure everyone was wearing their seatbelts. So I turned around and had the family get all belted up. Right after we turned a corner, there was another vehicle coming straight at us in our lane; it was a head-on collision, and we all survived because of those seatbelts!"

John was firm, "No, the seatbelts didn't save your life, *whatever told you to put them on* saved your life."

Probably a decade has passed since I heard John relate that story. Leaving a lasting impression on me, its message has deepened and taken on new meaning. The more experiences I have, the more profound the idea has become. He is right. It wasn't the seatbelts that saved their lives. True, they played a part in the actual physics of keeping the bodies secure during impact, but the credit belongs to the voice of warning. The "life-saving" seatbelts were there during the entire trip. But the timeliness of the prompting, *and the man's response to it,* changed the would-be tragedy into a miracle.

I am reminded of a game I played in high school. Planning to take some friends to a picnic, my friend and I prepared a tape recorder which described our every move as we traveled from our starting point to the final destination.

When it came time for the event, we told our unsuspecting friends to wait at a payphone until we called them and told them where to find the hidden tape recorder. Our instructions: "Turn it on and follow the directions explicitly!"

At the end of the journey was the picnic fit for a king. But along the way, we followed our friends, incognito. The most hilarious moments came when they tried to mimic what we had done, but in the wrong places. Having accidentally fallen out of step, our friends found that the description of our actions no longer suited their surroundings and, to us, it became absolutely laughable. If they had only known where they were trying to go, they could have improvised and found their own way without someone stepping in to point them in the right direction.

While this type of activity is good, clean fun for teenagers going to a picnic, it's an entirely different story when applied on life's journey to happiness. Yet, in actuality, this kind of nonsense happens all the time.

Sometimes we look at others who have reached an admirable destination in their life, and proceed to imitate the same steps that they took in an effort to achieve the same results. While we may learn a great deal from people who have what we want, we must realize that we are not always on the same sidewalk, so to speak, as they were on when they began *their* journey to the picnic. We also must not be so surprised when we end up with different results after duplicating their actions.

Have you ever seen the disclaimer attached to their success stories, "results not typical?" Believe me; I *know* that legitimate programs *are* truly fabulous, for I've had a number of them work wonders in my life. But, why *aren't* the results typical? What about the people who followed the directions perfectly but failed to enjoy remarkable results? How can we know if a "get wealthy," "get skinny," or "get happy" program is going to deliver in *our* life?

If we want the same results as someone else, we shouldn't so much *do* what they did, but rather learn how to *think* like they do. What they *did* may very well be exactly what is required to achieve the same success; but we each bring with us different life experiences, and a different variety of baggage. These elements make a difference in our results.

Therefore, we must discover the little voice inside of us that helps us get the direction and the *timing* right. If we have our eyes on the picnic table, and it is in clear view, then instinctively we will know how to get there. If we meet with an obstacle, and cannot make it on our own, then inspiration will lead us to the right tape recording designed perfectly for us, to take us from right where we are, to precisely where we want to be, at a pace that is right for us. We can enlist the "inner voice" to help us find our way simply by keeping a clear image in view of exactly where we're trying to go.

By learning to recognize the voice, and submitting to its advice, soon enough *we* become the latest success story and provide the next inspiring testimonial for the fabulous "get happy" program. Is the 'program' responsible for our success? Not any more than the seatbelt was exclusively responsible for saving the family from death.

Success comes as a result of preparing oneself for inspiration, and then being willing to pay attention to it and do what it says. I've learned that before I make big decisions, I must first have a clear picture in mind *and on paper* of the outcome *I* am seeking. What is the lifestyle I am after? In what kind of home do I want to live? What kind of relationships do I want with my family members? What kind of friends do I want to have? (Which picnic would I like to attend?) I must answer these questions in detail and actually commit the answers to paper. Then, and only then, do I look for the inspiration to direct me. *That* is when I'm ready to listen to and consider someone else's advice. *That* is when I am the student who is ready for the teacher to appear.

However, since every idea that comes our way may be either a proverbial life-saver, or actually the gate to a path of devastation, who can know the difference? It's therefore completely natural to be paralyzed with fear and remain with the misery which is familiar to us, rather than to take a risk and hope for the best.

The message in this book will teach you how to take the risk out of taking risks. You will be able to move forward with *confidence* in pursuit of your dreams. You'll know who to listen to, and you'll be able to trust what they say. In short, you'll be able to proceed methodically toward your worthy ideal, whatever it may be.

You might be thinking: *How could anyone be so certain?* If that's *your* question, this book is for you. This particular story is about one man's struggle to thrive financially, but the principles apply to any objective a person might have. Having enjoyed a measure of financial success with the principles contained in this book, I've also applied them to more trivial things, such as locating a roll of lost packaging tape in my utility closet, or obtaining the perfect parking spot in a time crunch. These principles are even effective in simply finding the answer to a pressing question on my mind. Bottom line, it works. All we have to know is what we really want. In other words, the first thing we must do is simply "pick our picnic," so to speak.

Following is a modern-day fable, or allegory. I've taken a brief analogy from another one of John W. Sims' dialogues and created a story around it so that its profound message will reach a greater audience and change lives for the better. What I have learned from John has certainly changed mine.

~ CHAPTER ONE ~
THE TROUBLE

"Richard, why can't you be more like your brother?" Felicity muttered as she flung the handful of envelopes across the bed. The bills were left strewn across the old patchwork quilt with the laundry piled next to them.

Pained by her comment, Richard pressed his lips together and swallowed hard. Clearly she was at the end of her rope. Again. "Felicity..." Richard sighed heavily. "Honey, I've been doing the best I know how." Richard slumped in the old recliner; his shoulders hung forward and he took a deep breath and closed his eyes. Then slowly opening them again, he glared at her from under his dark, thick eyebrows. "Besides, my brother is a crook. You really want to be married to a crook, huh? Well, sorry to break it to you, but I'm no crook. I'm just not."

"Crook or not, Richard, his kids have food on the table! And I don't believe all those stories about him anyway."

"Oh, come on. How else do you explain all that money?"

"I don't know. All I know is that I am tired of living like—like this." Felicity's throat tightened and her eyes closed. Suddenly she let out an angry noise and collapsed onto the bed, sending half of the bills sliding off the blanket and striking the floor on their corners like falling daggers.

Richard reached deep down and mustered one more attempt at moving forward. "Okay then, what should I do? Insurance? I've heard there's a lot of money in insurance. They say you can retire from selling it, and the money just keeps coming. What about that?" His voice was bland and it was obvious that this insurance idea did not thrill him. Still, he was searching for some hopeful idea that might finally please Felicity.

"Sales? I thought you said you were no crook." Felicity's brief, playful smirk was her own feeble attempt at lifting the mood in the room, a mood that she was responsible for ruining.

Richard was not amused. It took too much energy to respond the way he knew she wanted; this was supposed to be a serious conversation. "I've tried everything else, Felicity." He stared blankly at the floor in front of him. He felt weak and tired, but no emotion. It was killing him to face the facts of their financial condition and realize his powerlessness to do anything about it.

Just then the bedroom door that had been slightly ajar flew open and the doorknob banged on the wall next to Richard's chair. Richard didn't flinch, but Felicity shot an angry look toward little Matthew. Matthew didn't notice and scampered up onto Richard's lap. With the door wide open, the television could be heard in the kitchen as it played the whistling theme song to the Andy Griffith Show, which was having no positive effect on the cold feeling in the room.

Exasperated, Richard finally spoke with sudden rage. "Felicity, what the heck am I supposed to do?! I've done everything I've ever been told! I finished school because they (the proverbial committee) always said I'd need a degree to get a good job. I hired on with Wheeler because everyone said his company was growing so whoop-de-do fast that the profit sharing would blow our minds. I invested the LAST of our savings just the way Barry told me because HE'S done so well with the stock market. I bought this house because of all the HOOPLA that it was such a great deal. And now? NOW? Look at us! We're STILL eating oriental noodles once a day! Do you know how sick I am of NOODLES?! Let's just UP and MOVE TO CHINA for crying out loud! Oh yeah...we couldn't even SELL this dump if we WANTED to, because we OWE more than it's worth!"

Matthew sat frozen on his fathers lap. Neither Matthew nor Felicity was used to this kind of sarcasm coming from Richard. Felicity looked deeply into his eyes as he continued to fume, until he finally turned his face away from hers.

Under his breath, Richard continued, "And don't even mention that fiasco with my brother. All that money we spent and it just didn't work...for us, at least." He took a deep breath and shook his head, as if to shake off rising emotion and to steady his voice. More calmly he spoke, as if to himself, "How does Victor do it? I'm respectable, aren't I? That's all I can figure: the rich guys have GOT to be crooked, because the good guys like me get nowhere."

Felicity approached him and gently turned his face back to her, looking into his eyes. A new kind of fear washed over her. She realized this was the first time he had verbalized his defeat. Up until now, he had always gathered the strength to offer words of encouragement and hope. This time was different. Unconsciously tucking a loose strand of blonde hair behind her ear, she suddenly felt ashamed for the verbal beating she had given him. If only she could rewind this moment back just ten minutes, she could play the part she had expected him to play. But it was too late. What was that look on his face? What did it mean? What comes next? This was a scenario with which she was *not* familiar. Whatever happened to the predictable routine: wife feels discouraged, wife complains,

10

husband comforts wife and expresses confidence and determination to make things right?

Just then, Richard gripped Matthew's arms, and in one robotic motion stood up and put his four year-old on the bed next to his mother, forcing Felicity to step out of the way. Matthew also seemed perplexed by the deadpan look in his father's eyes, and looked at his mother, searching her face for a little reassurance. Had he done something wrong?

Richard left the room and mechanically picked up his jacket on his way through the kitchen and left through the side door. The door shut quietly.

Felicity looked at little Matthew as if he might have the answers to the questions spinning through her own mind. He was wide-eyed and of course didn't say anything, either. If Richard had slammed the door, she would have at least known that he was letting the last of his frustrations out, after which would have come about two hours of angry silence, followed by ten minutes of quiet co-habitation, followed by an "I'm sorry," a healing conversation, and a kiss. But this? This was new.

"Mommy, where's Daddy going?"

Felicity wondered the same thing but said, "Uh... he's probably just going to visit the neighbor."

Without another word, she slowly walked to the window. She could still make out his figure through the old-fashioned, warbled pane of glass; he was walking resolutely across their neighbor's pasture, but she perceived he was not headed toward their neighbor's house. She sat back down on the edge of the bed and observed, perplexed. In the other room the television rattled on unnoticed.

"...forecast through Wednesday is partly cloudy with temperatures ranging between 76 and 80 degrees..." The disregarded noise only added more muddle to the clutter already filling her head. "Breaking news...Local authorities have confirmed that the cause of death in the Upnow case was suicide..."

Suicide. Felicity hadn't even noticed the television was still on, but the word lingered in her mind nonetheless. She didn't even realize it was the television that planted the word in the first place. *Suicide?* Suddenly a new thought took root and she shuddered. *He wouldn't...no. Would he? Things aren't that bad, are they? Richard?* Felicity stood again and gently touched the window with her fingertips. She squinted and focused intently on the dark figure, now barely visible, as if a better look would help her know what Richard was thinking.

"Matthew, get your shoes, honey. We need to go for a walk."

12

~ CHAPTER TWO ~
REFLECTIONS

The wind blew softly through the pines as Richard glanced back over his shoulder at the pale-green farmlands disappearing behind him. He entered the breezy forest some fifty yards, searching for a secluded place which would be invisible from his little century-old home. *I just need to get away for a while. Clear my head.* He spotted a large, smooth, mossy rock about eighty more feet into the woods and walked towards it, carefully stepping over twigs and roots that encumbered his way. Upon reaching the rock, Richard squatted down and rested on its smooth, clean side. He rubbed his face slow and forcefully, as if it could push the financial stresses right out of his life somehow.

Lord, what do I do now? His thoughts were rhetorical. Richard gradually slid down until he was sitting on the ground, leaning back on the cold, hard rock. Pulling out his pocketknife and selecting a broken stick from the forest floor, he let out a heavy sigh and began fervidly scraping off some bark to the emphasis of certain words running through his mind. *I've DONE all I know. I DO what*

I'm told, and LOOK where it's put me. Everybody ELSE gets what they want, and I'M the failure. It's NOT fair! When do I get to be the one to have a little bit of good luck!?

Richard dropped his knife and hurled the stick as far as he could send it, causing it to ricochet off of the trunk of a quaking Aspen. He closed his eyes and reflected on the events of the last twelve months. He could still hear his brother just as clearly as the day it happened. "Ritchie, things are really moving. You realize I've already brought in eighty grand just this quarter? The time is right. You could make so much money with us. Buddy, your family needs this!"

"Victor, I know. It's just that I can't imagine talking to people and trying to sell anything, even if it is the greatest thing the world has ever seen."

"Look, it sells itself. How could you fail? You just do what the winners are doing and you'll win too! It's as simple as that."

Richard hesitated, then timidly expressed his perceived inferiority, "The winners have something I don't have, Victor."

Victor raised his eyebrows lovingly and shook his head. "What are you *talking* about, Ritchie? You're no different from them. Okay, maybe you could use a shot of self-confidence, but that isn't anything we can't help you with. What do you say? Just think, you start bringing in the kind

14

of money I'm talking about, and you can say 'sayonara' to your mortgage, huh?" Victor smiled and nudged Richard with his elbow. "Huh?" He repeated.

"I don't know, Vic."

"Tell you what. You come with me to the training meeting and after you see what kinds of people are making it, then you can decide."

~~~~~

There on the forest floor, Richard shifted his weight to relieve the pressure that the rock was inflicting to one side of his back. He smiled sardonically as he settled down again and recalled the meeting:

"Victor," Richard whispered discreetly. "Who *are* these people? They're *goofy,* for crying out loud."

Victor chuckled. "Ritchie, this is what I'm talking about. You see that guy over by the punch table?"

"You mean the one with the real nice suit and white sneakers?"

Victor laughed, "Yeah, that's the one." He leaned in closer and whispered, "He's a millionaire." He chuckled again, as if noticing the fashion faux-pas for the first time.

"NO."

"Honest, Ritchie. I *know* you can do it. You have a whole lot more going for you than most of these people, wouldn't you say?"

Richard was cautious to temper the excitement he felt inside. "A millionaire, huh?" Richard back-pedaled prudently, "I don't need a million, Victor. I just need enough money to pay my bills. And maybe enough so that someday I can send Matthew to college." His voice was reluctant but the glimmer in his eye was unbridled.

"Well, shoot, Ritchie. If they can make a million, then surely you could make enough to do that, don't you think?"

"Yeah, I think I could." There was a hint of courage and hope emanating through Richard's entire countenance now. "How much is it going to cost me to get started?"

~~~~~~

A squirrel rustled some leaves above his head, but Richard didn't flinch. By this time, Richard had his jaw cocked to one side as he shook his head slowly. If anyone had been with him there among the trees, he or she would have been smothered by the feeling of anger and cynicism which poured off of him.

Picking up a dirty stone, he rubbed it clean with his thumb. *It worked for Victor and the others, but not for me.* Settling, he concluded, *I didn't want*

16

to be like him anyway: all obsessed with riches. Money, money, money. Who needs it, anyway? I hate the stuff. I HATE it!

He chucked the stone and rubbed his eyes with the backs of his knuckles. Emotional exhaustion settled over him, and shifting his weight again he rolled to one side and eventually fell asleep. He heard the faint call coming from the neighbor's field, "Richard? Richard where are you?!"

Unconsciously he rolled slowly again to his back. But his answer, *"Honey, I'm just over here,"* stayed inside his own sleepy mind.

~ CHAPTER THREE ~
THE PATH

"There you are," his wife said, but only in his dream. Approaching him gracefully under the dappled sunlight that danced on her skin as it descended through the pines, she smiled and floated closer with her arms outstretched. In slow motion, she glided across the forest floor and then embraced him gently. He beamed as she kissed his cheek, and with an expression of adoration in her eyes she gently whispered, *"Now go and seek the fortune. I know you can do it."*

Richard stroked her hair lovingly and then touched her arm, smiling. "I'll do my best, dear. Don't you worry. Everything's going to be okay."

Felicity smiled back, her warm brown eyes glistening with melodramatic admiration for her man.

Proud to be the invincible hero, Richard confidently marched off in no particular direction, but did it with vigor nonetheless. In only a few short steps, the forest was gone and a worn-out road appeared before his feet. The pavement which must have at one time been a dark, shiny black color was now pale and spotted with potholes.

Surprised at its sudden appearance, Richard rubbed one of his temples and looked into the distance where the road seemed to be going. "Hmm. This has gotta go somewhere important...looks like a bazillion people have gone this way before. It's all worn out... That many people can't all be wrong. I bet I'll find just what I'm looking for." With that, he stepped onto the old road and began his journey.

Richard only walked what seemed to be a few short minutes when he noticed something. Up ahead on the road was a little, brown, paper bag. Curious, he pressed ahead and picked it up. It wasn't very heavy, and upon opening it he discovered a time card just like he had always used at his job with Wheeler's company. The top of it read, "Employment Incorporated," and underneath it was a blank line after the words, "Employee name." The paper sack also contained a little baggie with half of a peanut butter sandwich. He closed the sack, glanced around and saw no one. Should he consider this to be the good fortune he was seeking? It was somewhat sustaining, but not enough to meet the family's needs. Nevertheless, he opened the sack again, pulled out the sandwich, and continued walking. He downed the sandwich in only three bites and felt some degree of gratitude for the negligible success. "Wish it had been bigger, though." He sighed, and stuffed the baggie back into the paper sack. The timecard caught his eye again, but this time the blank line had his very own signature, "Richard Goodman." He frowned at the oddity of what had just occurred. But trying to find answers was futile as he was utterly alone on the path. The strangeness of this experience filled his head, and he strolled down the path, with his mind full of questions.

It wasn't long before he was hungry again, so the sight of another small, brown, paper sack along the road was encouraging. With renewed enthusiasm, he ran ahead and scooped it up, only to find that it was empty, aside from a folded "pink slip" with "Employment Incorporated" on the letter head, and one small baggie with crumbs from an already consumed sandwich. He stopped and squinted at the road that lay ahead and he thought he saw yet another sack.

Speeding forward with anticipation, he reached the third paper sack. It was more bulky than the first, actually. He opened it, and found another timecard with his name on it, and this time there was an entire peanut butter sandwich.

Then something else grabbed his attention. Curious, he searched into the distance along the ill-repaired road. Without shifting his gaze, he reached into the sack and slowly pulled out the sandwich as he continued to stare at the newfound images. A few other men had appeared up the road, walking away from him. He hadn't seen them

21

before, and wondered how he could have missed them. As he watched, almost magically more people began to materialize until there was quite a busy crowd, all traveling in the same direction. There must have been hundreds of them, robotically plodding along and picking up brown paper sacks.

Someone bumped him from behind, causing him to drop the sandwich. Richard turned as he heard the person apologize, "Oh, pardon me." He was taller than Richard and kept a quick and clumsy pace. In each hand were two paper sacks and a third was tucked under his arm. Before Richard could say a word, the man was gone. He had slipped ahead into the crowd and disappeared.

Richard reached down and retrieved the sandwich from the pavement, and then blew on it. He examined it briefly for any serious contaminants and glanced back up at the crowd where the awkward man had disappeared.

"What am I doing?" Suddenly he was conscious of the absurdity of the scene. The road that had seemed so promising...the hope that it would lead to a small fortune to take back to his family was clearly only going to provide just enough to keep him from ever changing his course. He dropped the sack, plopped down, defeated, right in the middle of the crumbling asphalt and put his head in his hands. Hoards of men now passed on either side of him. Each one was searching for another sack, hoping to find at least half of a sandwich. Some carried one sack; many carried two. Occasionally someone would pass by carrying three. The most frantic of the men were those who didn't have a sack yet, or those who carried a crumpled, empty one with a "pink slip" peeking out of the top.

Without warning, Richard was kicked in the hip by a slicked-haired man with wing-tipped shoes and a crisply pressed, pin-striped, button-up dress shirt. Without apology, the man stumbled on Richard but regained his footing and continued to race ahead, darting around people and glancing repeatedly at an athletic, blonde man in sweat pants and a tank top, sprinting nervously next to him.

"Oh come on, LOOK OUT, people!" The first man growled at everyone crowding his way. He shot an angry glance at the blonde man speeding along at his side and accidentally ran right into a curly headed stranger in a tweed blazer who had been unaware of the approaching fray. Refusing to go down, the slick-haired offender grabbed hold of the curly-head's shoulders, and thrust him, flabbergasted, into the path of his competitor.

"Ooof!" The blonde man was hit by the poor curly-headed stranger broadside and they both tumbled to the ground. "Aaaargh!" The blonde man punched the dusty path with the side of his clenched fist.

"I *told you,* It's *mine!*" The first man in wing tipped shoes pounced on the coveted brown paper sack which had apparently been the object of their obsession.

Richard was already standing again, having jumped up to avoid any other reckless pedestrians. Then approaching the blonde, Richard extended his hand to help him up, as well as the curly-head. The two men dusted themselves off and both slouched down the path, dejected: the stranger for the undeserved abuse he had just received, and the blonde for losing his chance to win the sack.

"Hey, mister! There're other sacks, you know." Richard called ahead to comfort the man.

The blonde stopped dead in his tracks turned around and looked sadly into Richard's eyes. "Call me Joe. Joe Bless. And no, there really aren't. I've looked for so long; I don't know when I'll ever see another sack. It's been so long since I've had one. Don't you see? *That* sack was the opportunity of a lifetime." The man turned away and scarcely lifted his feet as he disappeared into the crowd.

Richard squinted and looked up and down the path, eyeing at least thirty sacks placed sporadically along the road, just waiting to be retrieved. A lot of people seemed to pass them by without even a glance. Why did Richard see them, but Joe did not? Why was there such rudeness over obtaining the one bag for which the men fought? Such selfishness was so unnecessary!

Just then, a well-dressed woman walked by. She seemed to be thirty years old in Richard's estimation, give or take a couple years. She carried a diaper bag which hung from one elbow, a bulging laundry bag slung over one shoulder, a squirt bottle of disinfectant clipped to her hip, a purse over her other shoulder, a toddler girl in a backpack, a puppy under her arm...and a paper sack clutched in one fist.

Richard's mouth dropped open at the sight of the woman who lumbered by. He saw her twist an ankle in one of the dusty potholes. She winced but trudged on. She looked tired, and her little girl made brief eye contact with Richard. The babe's eyes held a look of weary longing. Her head was turned to one side with her cheek pressed gently against her mother's back. Blinking slowly, she then closed her eyes and snuggled into the warmth of her mother's back to take a nap.

He looked around at each of the men and women (now he saw many women) who flowed along the road where he still stood. He also noticed that, regardless of how many sacks they carried, they never turned around. They were continually pressing forward. He also saw that some women were trying to carry several children: one on their back, one on each hip...and a sack or two tightly in their hands.

But, the most heartbreaking of the images he saw were the women who had to put their children down. The mothers were doing all they could but found it utterly impossible to do it all. He heard one mother tell her little boy, "I'll find you a sandwich and bring it right back...just wait here for a little bit. I promise I won't be long." The child frowned and reached up to be held again by his mother, but she could only take one hand and kiss it, then turn away to find another paper sack.

Richard ached at the heartbreak of the little boy, as he thought of his own little Matthew. The boy slumped down on the rough asphalt and looked back just in time to see another young woman approach him, smiling. She was pulling a wagon full of toys, books, and musical instruments; and over her shoulder hung a duffle bag. The zipper was completely pulled open, and he could see that the bag was full of nearly eight or nine little brown paper sacks.

The next incomprehensible thing Richard saw sent a shudder down his spine. The woman reached down for the boy, and as if in slow motion, his color began to change and he literally began to morph as if straight out of an old sci-fi movie. *What the devil is happening?* Richard leaned closer to get a better look and blinked forcefully to clear anything from his eyes which could be causing the distorted image. The boy's soft, baby skin became rigid and then wrinkled and rough. The distinguishing characteristics of a child melted away and before Richard could grasp what was happening, the child shrank and became...*a paper sack*...the very moment the woman's hands took hold of him. She had a look of gratitude in her own tired eyes, gently placed the sack in her duffle bag with the others, and walked on.

Richard was stunned. *These children... Their own mother leaves, and they become someone else's paper sack?* The whole scenario was disturbing, and the ache he felt was almost unbearable. *This has got to be a dream... O-kaaaay, I'd really like to wake up now!* He slapped his cheeks to no avail. He slapped them again harder and was instantly sorry. Rubbing his cheeks, he thought the morphing child was certainly bizarre, but all he deeply cared about was returning to Felicity, and waking himself up wasn't working.

His stomach turned as he thought about having to get back to finding another sack. What good would it do? He could see that nobody ever seemed to turn back. How could they? They never found enough in those sacks to *ever* quit the insanity. And when a man came upon a weighty sack, loaded with more than the normal portion of peanut butter, jelly, and bread inside, it only

THE JACKRABBIT FACTOR/LESLIE HOUSEHOLDER

whetted his appetite for more and he would run quickly in search of another bonanza of sandwiches.

This is utterly insane! If I continue like them, I'll never get home. He shook his head and fought back tears of frustration that welled up in his eyes. Something deep inside told him he was meant for something greater than this. *There has to be a better way!* He wanted to turn around and reunite with his wife, but he had nothing to bring her. *I need to find something enduring,* he thought.

Richard closed his eyes and tried to imagine, tried to *create* a solution in his mind. It was about the toughest thing he had ever done: directing his thoughts toward some unknown, unidentified, answer.

Instinctively he felt he had some kind of genius idea hidden somewhere within. But his mind was inclined to wander, to think about the images of the people that thronged about him on either side...or to think about what his wife could be doing at that moment...or reflect on the paper sacks and their meager contents. But, with each temptation to let his thoughts drift, he consciously forced himself to search hard and deep for a brand NEW idea...

...but nothing came to mind. Richard let out a frustrated sigh and opened his eyes. Strangely, he was alone. Did just the mere effort of trying to think differently from the crowd set him apart from the others, in a very literal sense? Everyone was gone! This state of affairs was absolutely confusing to Richard, until he remembered something his father had said more than once: "There is no labor from which most people shrink as they do from that of sustained and consecutive thought. It is the hardest work in the world." *Now who said that? Oh yeah, there's a name I could never forget. Wallace Wattles. Wa-, Wa-, WOW...*Richard laughed to himself. *Who was that guy anyway?* Richard's mind meandered. Then he thought again about his father's words, and he realized, *Thinking is hard work, isn't it Dad. I know there's got to be a solution here; I just don't know what I'm looking for.*

Richard's father had been pretty well off. He was a quiet man, but had built a beautiful life for his family. He seemed to be such an ordinary fellow, but lived the life of a closet millionaire. Not a showy life, but an abundant one, nonetheless. He drove modest but quality cars and had a small home that was furnished elegantly and beautifully kept. He traveled to exotic destinations and returned with interesting gifts from the Orient and Europe. If he hadn't passed away so early, Richard might have been more conscious of what his father was really all about. Victor was five years older than Richard, and had spent long hours talking with their father, gleaning the wisdom and insight that accompanies a millionaire mentality. Unaware that such a thing existed, Richard was beginning to realize that until now, he hadn't known *there was more to know.*

Richard answered his father out loud, "Dad, I don't even know what I am looking for!"

"What do you *want?*" His father's voice spoke in Richard's mind.

What do I want?

~ CHAPTER FOUR ~
THE FEAR

As Richard slept by the rock, Felicity and Matthew searched on, over the rocks and roots of the forest floor. They still called for him but he could no longer hear their voices. The thickness of the woods hid him from their sight, even though he slept only a stone's throw away.

"Richard?!"

"Daddy!" Matthew called. Then turning to his mother he asked, "Where's Daddy? Why are we in the forest?"

Felicity didn't know how to answer so she changed the subject. "Matthew, how are you, honey? You doin' okay?"

"I'm okay, Mommy. But my feet hurt." He raised a foot as if to show her the evidence.

"I'm sorry, sweetheart." She squatted down and briskly rubbed his pant leg. Slowly she turned around, shaking her head. Talking to herself she quietly muttered, "Which way do we go? How on earth do I find him in here?"

"Can I sit down, Mom?"

"Sure, honey. Let's rest a minute." They sat together on a fallen log and she closed her eyes to say a silent prayer that everything would be okay.

Felicity felt a little better, more assured that they would find Richard all right, but she quickly began second guessing her impressions of peace. *What if I'm wrong, what if he's already given up, what if Matthew sees him first, and he's—?* Her imagination began to run wild. *What if we're too late?* Her body tensed with fear and she jumped up, startling her little boy, and yelled, "Richard!" She didn't mean to frighten Matthew so she quickly adjusted her demeanor. She also decided she needed to go back for help.

"Hey, I have a good idea, let's go take your shoes off at home and give your precious little feet a break, okay?" Felicity's voice was shaky, but falsely cheerful as she tried to hide how worried she felt. It even cracked a bit, but Matthew apparently didn't notice. Scooping her four-year old into her arms, she hurried as best as she could back toward the farmlands. Her small, five-foot three frame struggled under his weight as she tried not to stumble on the uneven ground beneath her feet. Soon they were back in her old kitchen.

Taking off his shoes she said, "Oh, sweetie, look at the clock. We're late for your nap." Matthew was tired anyway, and Felicity needed to think.

She let him have a drink and tucked him into his toddler bed.

Felicity kissed him and then closed his door. With no little eyes watching her, she surrendered to her anxieties and became frantic. She scrambled for the phone and it fumbled out of her hands and landed under the table. Reaching down to pick it up, and having to crawl partially under the table, she pushed against the chair, which became stuck against the table leg and finally fell over. She growled, and her tightly frowning eyebrows raised a little as she tried to see the numbers through the tears pooling in her eyes.

Leaving the tipped chair on the yellowed linoleum where it lay between the table and faded avocado green couch, Felicity put the phone to her ear and paced the floor in front of the little table. "Hello, police? Um, my husband is gone; we *really* need to find him!"

"How long has he been missing, ma'am..."

"Uh, I don't know," Felicity looked in vain for a clock on the wall, or a watch on the counter, or anything to help her have some kind of reference. "I don't know, maybe an hour..."

"Can I have your name, please?"

"Felicity Goodman."

"Felicity, is there a reason why you are concerned after only an hour?"

"Well, he was upset. He left without saying anything. He never does that! I just don't know what he's going to—where he's—what I—" Felicity stammered, realizing that the operator did not feel the panic that she was trying to convey.

"Please calm down, Mrs. Goodman. Do you have any idea where he might have gone?" Her inquiry was obviously a routine statement rather than a question motivated by genuine concern.

"He went into the woods behind my house."

"I've started a statement here, but to be honest with you we cannot file it as an official missing persons report until he has been gone at least twenty-four hours."

"Twenty-four hours!? What if that's too late? What about—I don't know, isn't there anything you can do?"

"If he were a minor, it would be different. But the policemen on staff can't place a high priority on a case like this because, frankly, most of the time the person has left of his own free will and will *also* return on his own before the twenty-four hours is up."

Felicity was speechless.

"Mrs. Goodman?"

"Uh, yeah...um..." Felicity didn't know what to say but didn't want to hang up yet either. Surely she could say something to change the outcome of the phone call. She finally spoke to the dispatcher,

"Uh, well, what do you suggest I do? I'm afraid he might...try something." She couldn't seem to say the word *suicide* because she didn't want to believe it could really be true. Speaking it out loud to the operator would have taken this nightmare out of her head and straight into reality somehow. It would have seemed so serious. She sort of hoped this whole day was just a bad dream.

"Felicity, do you have reason to believe he is in danger?" Again her question came out like a statement.

"Well, yes, and no... he's never threatened... suicide... or anything, but he was so depressed looking, and he left without an explanation."

"Would you like me to send out an officer to talk with you and get the paperwork started, at least?" The operator seemed to be demonstrating a little more compassion.

Felicity was relieved. Albeit not the kind of help she hoped for, she thought it might be comforting to have the officer come, anyway. Even a little bit of attention from the authorities would be better than nothing. The emptiness she felt inside was gnawing at her nerves. It must have been her tendency toward comfort food as well as the thought of a police officer coming over in a black and white car with lights on top that instilled a sudden craving for a nice, white, jelly-filled doughnut.

37

After giving the operator the needed information, Felicity hung up the phone and stepped over to the window again. She gazed across the farmer's fields and into the woods. They seemed so impenetrable from that far away. They looked shadowy and harsh. *Where are you, Richard? Where are you?*

It took the officer about forty-five minutes to arrive at her home. As she waited, she searched her nearly empty cupboards for something edible to help her feel better. She wasn't the least bit hungry, but eating would calm those nerves. She finally found some graham crackers and prepared to whip up some icing sugar and milk to spread across the top.

After clearing a place at the table, she began to put it all together. Her hands shook, while she thought so much, in detail, about the horrible things that Richard was probably experiencing. The depression, the anger, the loneliness, the hopelessness...and the suicide! She envisioned the funeral and how Matthew was going to have to deal with the loss of his father!

Felicity absent-mindedly stirred the icing mixture. Her mind wasn't on crackers or icing or even the chair still lying on its side by the couch. After pouring a glass of milk she dunked a corner of the cracker, swishing it back and forth until the edge of the two sandwiched crackers became heavy and soft. Briefly allowing the excess milk to drip off, she lifted the crackers to her lips, and consumed most of the soggy clump. A small section that broke off too soon rolled down her chin and onto her blouse. Leaving it there, she only looked down on it; then, seeing it as evidence that her life truly was falling apart, her brows furrowed and the tears returned full force. Leaving the rest of the crackers on the table, she picked up the small bowl of icing. Dipping her finger in, she walked to the couch and then buried the glob of icing in her mouth. Before she knew it she had eaten the whole batch.

Disgusted, exhausted, and scared, she set the bowl down on the floor and reclined on the couch. She was just curling into a fetal position when the doorbell rang. She began to jump to her feet as she shouted, "Come in!" Losing her balance she fell off the couch, banging her knee on the fallen chair. Struggling to her feet, she kicked the chair, just as the concerned officer and his partner were swinging the door wide open. Felicity's other foot was caught in one of the rungs and she began to lose her balance.

"Lady?!"

Felicity's hands flew out in front of her, preparing to catch herself if in case she toppled all the way down to the floor. Then waving them backwards full circle like windmills, she finally stabilized herself. Standing erect, she prudently brushed the wrinkles from her blouse, unknowingly leaving the soggy graham cracker stuck to her chest. "I was, uh, just..." Felicity drew a blank and finally just sighed, resigned to an idiotic first impression.

"May we come in?"

Recovering, she said, "Yes, yes, please come in."

Relieved by their long-awaited arrival, Felicity fought back a new release of tears which she valiantly kept at bay...for a few moments. Then failing, she rubbed them away, smearing her cheap mascara as it ran in black streams down her cheeks.

The officers watched her, uncertain about what they were getting themselves into. The thin layer of crusty icing around her mouth looked like the remains of a dreadful froth that had all dried up. The senior officer glanced down at the chair, then back to her.

Embarrassed, Felicity stepped her foot out from between the chair rungs, kicked it behind her and motioned for the officers to come in.

Senior Officer Cross chose not to call further attention to the disarray. The poor woman was obviously distraught, and he just wanted to get down to business. His junior partner glanced at him, and in response, the senior officer discreetly shook his head with a slow blink, meaning, "Never mind all of this."

But before the senior officer proceeded with his duties, he glanced once more at the chair. He *was* a little surprised that she hadn't merely picked it up.

"Ma'am, can I get some more information about your, um, husband?"

Felicity nodded and let him sit at the small kitchen table. She pushed the radio and crackers to one edge so he would have more room to spread out the paperwork. Junior Officer Doolittle remained standing behind Cross, and Felicity sat back on the couch not far from her visitors.

Cross, the senior officer, looked intently and directly at her; and squinting, he cocked his head to one side. He found it hard to overlook the raccoon eyes, the streaks of tears turned black with mascara, and the dried froth. The dispatcher had briefed him that this was not an urgent case, so why was this poor woman such a wreck? Finally he spoke, "Ma'am, how long has he been missing?"

"Um," she sniffed, "about two hours..." She noticed he wasn't looking her in the eyes. Was he looking at her mouth? Self-consciously, Felicity tried to wipe her mouth with the back of her wrist. She glanced at the younger officer with him, who was a little uninterested, eyeing the rest of the milk and iced crackers.

Cross leaned back in the chair and his shoulders relaxed. "Ma'am, don't you suppose that he might just be out for a walk?"

How could she answer that? She was choking back sobs. Trying to speak would have only sounded like the emotional high pitched words of a little girl. The patronizing tone of the policeman's words made her feel small. Felicity shook her head slowly, but she didn't say a word.

~ CHAPTER FIVE ~
THE INSTRUCTION

Against the cold, hard rock, Richard continued to doze. In the tree above him slithered a snake that had just caught view of the solitary man below. Slowly and quietly it crept toward a lower branch, and then paused.

The breeze was cool, but the sun shone through a gap in the trees and kept his body warm. In the meantime, his mind was far away, taking in the strange scenes of the potted road and amber fields. He once again heard his father's voice speak, "What do you *want*? Richard, our minds are powerful tools. Your thoughts are alive and *do* more than you realize. Don't be careless with your thoughts." Richard suddenly felt like he wasn't alone. He turned, and there stood his father, smiling.

"Dad?" The last time Richard laid eyes on his father was when he was only twelve. Unfortunately, those final memories were tainted with the dismal images that accompanied his father's final battle with cancer. He almost didn't recognize his father standing there so alive and robust; he appeared to have the strength and health of a young man in his prime.

In his younger days, Richard's father had been a brilliant businessman. So Richard had been told, anyway. What does that mean to a kid? But because cancer had cut his father's life too short, Richard, with his mother and seventeen year-old brother, was left behind.

"Son," his father smiled and opened his arms.

"Oh, Dad..." Richard melted into his father's arms just as he had dreamed over and over. When he felt alone or depressed, he often closed his eyes and visualized this very event. "Dad, I have missed you *so* much...You're here! How—?" Richard exclaimed through breathy sobs.

"Ritchie. Oh, my little Ritchie. I've been with you, on occasion, but you couldn't see me. At times, your thoughts drew me close to you. Just as the things you desire. That is what I am here to tell you now: You want money? Use your thoughts. You need food? Use your thoughts. Think on the worthy desires of your heart, and they are drawn to you spiritually."

"What do you mean, Dad?" Richard pulled away from his father's embrace, but continued to hold his arms.

"All physical things have a spiritual counterpart. By thinking, we draw the spiritual counterpart to ourselves. By persisting in right thought, the angels do our bidding and arrange the affairs of men to cause the worthy desires to pass from the spiritual to the physical world."

Richard's brows furrowed and he shook his head slightly. "That seems too simple, and kind of weird, Dad. I've thought lots of things that never came true."

"As long as you believed it was coming, the dream was actually on its way. All things in the universe that were required to see the dream come true were gathering for your benefit. However, and this is where most men fail, the moment you entertain doubt or fear, all of those forces reverse and the things, the ideas, the situations, the people you need immediately draw away from you."

His father paused, and then continued, "Our negative thoughts actually and literally cause the blessings to be repelled. If you can picture what you want, and believe that it is on its way, by God's law it must come. Hold on to the belief, and in time you will realize it." Richard's father panned the area surrounding them, and held up his hand as if to display the scenery to his son. "The earth is abundant with all that any man could desire. But by his own misuse of thought he cannot see it." He dropped his hand and then tapped Richard's forehead, "Change your thinking, and you will see the opportunities all around you. You have been blind to them, but they are all around you right now."

Blind to them? Richard thought about the blonde man who couldn't see the sacks. *What am I missing? What's all around me now that I can't see?* Richard looked around. He wasn't sure what he was looking for but nothing really stood out. He saw the dilapidated road, the vast fields on each side, the tree line and thick forest in the distance. He looked back at his father, puzzled.

"Son, you have to know what you want. If someone else has what you want, learn from them, but you must trust your own instincts to make the right decisions. The voice of inspiration will come only after you have a clear picture in your mind of what *you* are seeking, and *after* you allow yourself to feel truly grateful, as though you already enjoy the success."

This philosophical stuff wasn't making much sense to Richard. It seemed terribly vague, and hardly useful. Along this path, many things had been bizarre; this odd conversation was no different. So he didn't take it too seriously and simply nodded graciously to his father. "Thanks, Dad."

"Now go. Know what you want, and when you find it, chase it. You'll know what to do."

Richard blinked and lifted his eyes, nodding as though he was committing the advice to memory. But before he could thank his father again, the kind, wise gentleman disappeared.

Richard spun around to see where his father had gone, but he was alone. With a sentimental sigh, he paused and then looked again at the road. "What do I want? I wanna wake up already!" Then with a groan, he lamented, "I want food for my family. I want to go home to my wife and Matthew." He looked down the road in each direction, a little confused because he could not remember from which direction he had come. He saw a few footprints in the dirt where the asphalt had completely worn through. They all were pointed in one direction, so he chose to go the same way.

Somewhere off the path, something rustled the tall grass. Richard jumped, startled by the sudden noise. The tall, golden, wheat-like grass swayed in the light breeze, and all was quiet. In one spot, maybe fifty feet away, he saw a gap in the grass where something hid. In an instant he heard another rustle, and the gap was gone.

~ CHAPTER SIX ~
THE INSANITY

Immediately, coming from the hole in the grassy field, he heard the warning growl of an angry, agitated wild dog. *Oh, please, no...*Sickened by the sudden rush of adrenaline, Richard froze. The dog snarled and leapt up out of the grass and landed again, out of sight. After a tense moment of silence it appeared again, barked, growled, and then darted one way and then the other, in a crazed way. Richard relaxed just a bit as he realized the dog hadn't seen him after all, but decided to move cautiously down the road away from the rabid-looking beast. The wolf-like dog was undoubtedly insane...his mouth dripped with saliva and his glowing yellow eyes had Richard entirely unnerved.

But before Richard could move, he saw the dog was already headed *straight* for him, so he took off like a rocket. Panting, he ran as fast as he could, and escaped into the field on the opposite side. He hurdled dirt mounds and whipped through the tall, brown grass. Stealing a brief glance behind him he saw the dog approach within ten feet...and immediately dart *away* just as quickly.

Richard pounded the dusty ground with his loafers as he slowed to a stop and tried to catch his breath. Leaning over with his hands on his knees, and between gasps, he raised one eyebrow and squeaked out a breathy, "…Huh?"

Why did the dog turn around, Richard wondered in his mind, *Is there something worse lurking somewhere?* Nervously, Richard looked about and searched for hidden danger. There was nothing nearby that could have frightened the dog. Richard was absolutely stumped. The growling and the barking continued, and the dog literally hopped from place to place in frenzy. *That's it. The dog's insane.* Returning to the road, Richard tiptoed along with a quicker pace and kept one eye on the dog for his own safety. In and out of the grass, the dog continued growling, foaming, and snarling back and forth, up and down. *Poor dog. I wish someone would put it out of my misery.* He chuckled at his witty thought then proceeded cautiously down the path, feeling safer after determining that although the dog was crazy it seemed harmless enough.

As he turned from the dog, he thought about the visit from his father. He smiled to himself and relived the warmth of his father's genuine love.

His moment of peace, however, was interrupted abruptly by the appearance of the same wacky dog which had now stumbled out into the road immediately in front of him. The dog re-

50

established its footing and with a rabbit in its mouth, glanced placidly at Richard and walked peacefully away into the grass on the other side of the road.

Richard paused and cocked his head to one side. *A rabbit? It was chasing a rabbit this whole time!?* He chuckled out loud at his misconception. The dog had been chasing a rabbit. Suddenly it all made sense. The dog wasn't crazy, and it wasn't rabid. Richard recalled all of the jumping and growling, the darting to and fro...he laughed at himself for being anxious and making such a judgment.

"Oooooh, I'd like to have a rabbit, too..." Someone spoke from behind. Richard turned around, taken aback by the sudden company.

"Yeah, a rabbit would be nice. Much better than all those peanut butter sandwiches, eh? M'name's Richard. What's yours?" Richard extended his hand to the small, round man now standing next to him with a five o'clock shadow and somewhat disheveled comb-over.

The man didn't break the stare he had fixed on the dog as it sauntered away, but politely replied, "Harold. Harold Ashway." He exhaled slowly and sighed, "I want one of those rabbits." Harold's face lacked expression. He seemed to be awestruck by the sheer memory of the prize.

Without another word, the man stepped off the road into the sheaves of grass and jogged clumsily ahead about forty feet. Then with a wave of his hand and a smile in Richard's direction, he turned and began to leap around as if he was chasing some kind of elusive rabbit. *Except...there was no rabbit.*

Richard squinted. *What in the chickens is he doing...?*

The man paused, scratched his head and then got down on his hands and knees, whereupon he started darting around like an animal on all fours; and then to top it all off, he actually started barking. And growling! Barking and snarling and jolting all over the place, the man carried on and Richard's mouth dropped wide open. *Oh...my...word. You've got to be kidding me.* Richard tried his best to make sense out of the man's odd behavior. It was as though he was imitating the dog's actions without even seeing something to chase, thinking he would gain a rabbit by doing so. What was he barking at, anyway? *Does the fool think that copying a crazy dog's gonna somehow PRODUCE a rabbit? Oh, PLEASE! There's no rabbit! And even if there was one out there somewhere, he'd be scaring it away!!!*

"Harold Ashway! If you carry on like that...!"

Richard paused when he caught sight of three or four jackrabbits right behind the man, frightened by all the commotion. The man was oblivious to them; he never even heard them scamper away, nor did he pay attention to Richard's exclamations. Richard attempted to hold back the laughter he felt rising in his chest but failed to hold back the one massive grunt that escaped through his nose. Rubbing the back of his neck, he turned away to leave the man to his business.

Just then his father's voice returned to his mind, "Know what you want, and when you find it, chase it. You'll know what to do."

Richard began slowly walking down the path again, rehearsing his father's words and contemplating the ludicrous scene he had just witnessed.

Then he thought about his brother, Victor. He remembered all the things people had said about him, how crazy he was, how he'd burn the candle at both ends...and how doing the same things had never produced the same results for Richard.

Richard stopped dead in his tracks. That last thought sunk into the deepest recesses of his soul, and he clapped his hand to his mouth. *I was always trying to do what Victor did in order to get what he got. I've **always** tried to do what someone else did to get what they got, but it **doesn't** work that way, does it, Dad? I was actually scaring away any* *success that might have been nearby! Just doing what someone else has done is like copying the crazy dog, isn't it?*

Richard thought deeply about this new perspective. He thought about the way he should behave in order to get different results. It seemed so simple, philosophically, at least. He realized that, first of all, he needed to be calm and confident. But how could he be confident when he had doubts about so many things? Well, he wasn't sure about that; he just knew that he needed to find a way. He knew that to catch a rabbit, he *had to be* calm or they would detect him and disappear. He needed somehow to *attract* to him the thing that he wanted, because it was clear that busy-ness without focus would be a waste of time.

What did he want? *A rabbit would be nice,* he thought. It would be something he could take home to his family and they could make stew. That would be much better than all the sandwiches he had found. He stepped off the path and sat down on an old, dried up stump, scoping the area for any rabbits. Nothing.

Opportunities all around me, huh? He began to feel cynical again. Shaking his head he looked over his shoulder and studied the old road again. With a heavy sigh, he stood up and decided to speculate some more after gathering another sandwich. He needed the energy. After all, this thinking business was tough, exhausting stuff.

He plodded along, and before he knew it he was shoulder to shoulder with hundreds of men and women in search of brown paper sacks once again. But this time all of the crowds annoyed him more than ever. He knew better. He knew there was a way to leave the hordes in the mindless quest for mediocrity. *Oliver Wendell Holmes...Didn't he say that, "A mind once stretched by a new idea never regains its original dimension?"* Now he understood why the sack-race was so intolerable to him now. Never did that saying mean as much as it did now. He could not stand this way of life, knowing that something better was waiting for him.

In fact, he was sure he hadn't noticed them before, but occasionally he spotted individuals out in the field, well off the beaten path, who strode along in the opposite direction. Each of them had an aura of confidence and hurried anticipation as they rushed alongside of, but against, the crowd.

Where were they going? It didn't take long for Richard to deduce that they were on their way home to their families, because they each carried a captured rabbit. On top of that, behind them was gathering a small but growing handful of rabbits, appearing from nowhere and following these people like the rats in the story of the Pied Piper.

Richard nudged a man who was walking next to him. The man glanced over with a questioning look.

"Did you see that?" Richard threw a thumb in the direction of the latest rabbit captor.

"See what?"

"The people with the rabbits."

"Oh, them. Yeah, I notice those kinds of people every once in a while, and I swear they are so irritating."

"Irritating?"

"Yeah, now and then they stop to get on the path right in front of me."

"NO! Serious? Why would they do that?"

"I think they get a kick out of being annoying. They get in my face with all this talk about how I could have my own rabbit," the man chuckled. "I mean really, when would I ever have time to catch myself a rabbit with so much to do here on the path? I wish they'd just leave me alone."

"So what do you tell them?"

"I tell them that they are full of baloney and to get out of my way. I've always known that if something sounds too good to be true, it probably is."

Richard didn't say anything. He kept pace with the man and remained silent for a while. Finally, he had to know, "What if they really *could* show us how to get a rabbit? Wouldn't you want one? Don't you have a family you could go back to if you had one?"

"Oh, sure I have a family. But it's my job to collect sandwiches until I retire. I've only got about twenty years left of this."

That thought was painful to Richard. "Wouldn't you want a rabbit?"

"Oh, see, that's just too good to be true. I could never get a rabbit. In fact, I don't think I am supposed to have one, anyway."

"Why is that?"

"God said I can't go to heaven if I get a rabbit."

"What? What are you talking about?"

"He said that rabbits are the root of all evil."

"No, He didn't."

"Oh, yes He did. And if you'll excuse me..." The man became nervous and hurried away from Richard.

"The root of all evil?" Richard whispered to himself.

Richard attempted to run the man's logic through his own head. Here was a man planning to spend the next twenty years away from his family, with most of that time in pursuit of little brown paper sacks because it was taboo to find a rabbit. So, *was* it wrong? Was he on some forbidden quest that would alienate him from the Source of all good? He didn't want a rabbit for the sake of having a rabbit, he wanted one because it would make it possible for him to return with complete focus to his family.

Looking at the panorama of individuals in perpetual search for sandwich after sandwich, Richard couldn't help but wonder what was going on in the lives of their families back home. Did they have any idea what they were missing? *Do I have any idea what I am missing? What would it be like to be a room parent at school in Matthew's class next year? I wonder what a room parent does, anyway. And then there's Felicity. Wouldn't my marriage thrive and grow like never before if I had the time, means, and freedom to continue developing that relationship the way I really want? If my family is the most important thing to me, am I spending most of my time developing those relationships? Uh, NO! I'm spending all of my time looking for stupid sandwiches in dad-blasted paper sacks!* Richard suddenly yelled out loud, "The root of all evil?!" *I just want to go home. I just want a rabbit so I can finally be home.*

Was that so wrong? Maybe so. Maybe he was supposed to engage in the sack-race his whole life if for no other reason than to build his character. After all, that's what everybody else does. Stick with the program. Don't deviate. Do what you're told, and you'll succeed. A little bit of fear spread over him as he spotted a sack and numbly picked it up.

He decided to put the whole rabbit idea away for a while. It was too conflicting and frankly, a nagging nuisance. He *knew* that was what he wanted, but there was just too much of a mental wrestle to try to do anything about it.

The crowds of people around him became thicker. Pretty soon he couldn't move without bumping someone. He was in a veritable foot-path traffic jam. Richard groaned inside as he came to terms with the fact that unless he chose to think differently from the crowd, he would only drown in the floods of mediocrity, and probably perish from the conscious awareness of his own failure to achieve his dream. Would he miss the chance to enjoy watching Matthew grow up? How long would his wife keep holding on to the hope that he'll one day accomplish what he set out to do?

The thought of disappointing Felicity was more than he could bear. He stopped abruptly and realized that it was too late for him to ever be satisfied with keeping step with the crowds. He closed his eyes and held still. For a short time he was bumped over and over from the masses that pressed on. Once in a while the blow was so abrupt and forceful that it almost knocked him over, but he didn't flinch.

He envisioned his wife smiling at him, and his little Matthew running to jump into his arms. These were the images that brought him joy. He could hear Felicity say, "Oh, honey, you *did* it. I knew we could count on you." With his eyes still closed, he relished her adoration and could feel the joy that swelled up inside from reuniting with his loved ones...

...and the crowds were gone.

~ CHAPTER SEVEN ~
THE TRAGEDY

Silently, Felicity felt her mind slip into a fog. This wasn't going right. She had very real concerns, and who could she turn to if the police weren't going to take her seriously? They just glared at her; what could she do? She couldn't even speak to them without feeling like a fool.

Whether or not my fears are justified, I deserve at the very least an empathetic ear! Who's going to help me? Who'll listen to me, and convince me that everything is okay? Who'll change the way I feel?! Who'll save me from this nightmare?!

Exhaling forcefully, Officer Cross displayed his impatience. "Ma'am, if you are not going to talk to me, there isn't a whole lot I can do for you."

If you're not going to treat me with some respect, then I'm not going to talk to you.

"So what's it going to be?" Cross glowered at Felicity with his eyes half closed, and his eyebrows raised high. He glanced at his junior partner who stood apprehensively near the wall. The younger Officer Doolittle seemed to want to say something to break the tension, but showing Felicity any compassion at this point would be undermining the arrogant superior, and would undoubtedly be met later with a reprimand.

Still refusing to respond, Felicity looked at the floor defiantly and prayed for some kind of advocate to save her from the humiliation she felt growing inside.

Cross knew what would change the stalemate. "Perhaps you know *exactly* where your husband is, and you just don't want to tell us what happened, is that it?"

Felicity finally looked up, incredulous. Cross stared her down, searching for any hint of guilt in her response. She crumpled her eyebrows, closed her eyes and shook her head, whispering, "This can't be happening to me..."

~ CHAPTER EIGHT ~
THE DIFFERENCE

Richard opened his eyes and saw that the group had vanished. He turned around, looking to see where they had gone but they were nowhere to be seen. *Whoa,* Richard thought. *That was easy.* He took mental note that if he ever felt crowded among the masses of mediocre minds, he needed only to close his eyes and imagine what he wanted, and most importantly, imagine the *feelings* that would go with it. He guessed that most people never take the time to really do that.

He noticed a sack at his feet. With a new attitude toward it, realizing that it wasn't his ultimate goal, he nevertheless felt a degree of reverent gratitude that it was there. He looked heavenward and thought, *Thank you for this. It gives me the energy I need to pursue my goal.* He reached down, picked it up and carefully pulled it open. Smiling, he pushed aside the timecard and pulled out a triple-decker sandwich.

A voice inside his head spoke to him, *"Ah, you keep on this path and the sandwiches will just get bigger and bigger! See? All you need is patience and persistence and you'll get all that you need right here on this path..."*

~~~~~~

In the forest where Richard slept, the serpent lifted its head and quietly loomed over him. Suddenly a thin twig cracked and fell, dropping the baleful creature next to his arm. It crept up his sleeve and then settled onto his chest. It remained poised, hovering over his shirt pocket, gazing at Richard's face.

~~~~~~

In his dream, Richard paused to think. He looked down the path, as if to somehow determine whether the voice was telling the truth. Would he really find all he needed along this road? But instead of seeing sacks, he began to see people again. *No, that's just what everyone else thinks. I need to think differently than the others. I have to think DIFFERENTLY.*

It bothered him a little that he wasn't alone on the path anymore. He felt like he must be slipping into popular mentality for them to show up like they did. He closed his eyes again and imagined his family. He thought about standing near his back porch in the thick, cool, green turf, and picking up Matthew and twirling him in the air. He saw the trees zoom past behind his son as

Matthew giggled and thrust his head back in sheer delight. Even with his eyes closed, Richard's thoughts put a real smile on his face and upon opening his eyes once again, he found himself completely alone.

There. Now, where was I?

He stepped off the path, and sat on an outcropping of rocks about ten feet from the road. He was consciously aware that thinking and feeling the happy images actually set himself apart from the crowds. Now, he began to wonder what it might be that he should do next to get a rabbit. *Use my thoughts, huh, Dad? I wonder what he meant by that.*

He closed his eyes and imagined a rabbit in front of him. Richard found this difficult, as he wasn't good at keeping his thoughts from darting all over the place. But he managed to see in his mind an outline of a small, gray animal with tall ears. The shape of the creature was sort of abstract for the brief moment that it was the dominant image. It seemed dark all around and almost like a watermark, nothing more.

But he *did* hear a rustle. Richard opened his eyes and looked out into the distant field. He was certain he saw the tall grass move in one particular spot. All of the grass was swaying in the mild breeze, but in one place something seemed to be hiding.

He stood up cautiously, and saw it: a small animal with two long ears, far away and somewhat vague. But he saw it!

He fixed his eyes on the animal and slowly, vigilantly approached it.

It was impossible to move through grass without making noise, so it wasn't long before the rabbit looked his way and immediately darted toward the woods at the edge of the field.

"Aaaargh! There's no way I'm going to be fast enough to catch a rabbit like that!" Richard threw his hands up and let them fall to his side.

He moaned and returned to his perch on the rocks. He looked back to the path, feeling a little lonely. *There's nobody out here, at least the path never lacked company when you wanted some.* He shouted out loud, "At least I wasn't alone in my misery!"

Richard moped for a while. Finally he muttered to himself, "What am I doing? Who do I think I am, anyway? I'm no Victor. I don't know how to do this."

He looked up just in time to see a smiling man holding a rabbit by its ears. Lifting it up, he greeted Richard as he passed by, about thirty feet away, well off the worn-out path.

The voice in his head spoke up, *"Oh, would you look at the showoff...What a jerk. He's just rubbing it in your face that you don't have a rabbit."*

But Richard reserved judgment. He acknowledged the impish voice, but he wasn't choosing to believe it, not yet.

Richard waved his hand to return the greeting and forced a smile. The man jerked his head to one side, a gesture that invited Richard to come along. Richard glanced around to determine if the invitation was truly for him, or intended for someone else. When he saw no one else around, he shrugged and stood up to join the rabbit man.

Something about him was magnetic. He seemed so self-assured. So at peace with himself. So directed. Richard wanted to be like that. He wanted to know what the man knew. He wanted to know how to catch a rabbit.

"Good day," the rabbit man greeted.

"Good day." Richard responded.

"I saw you sitting in the field, and thought you might be interested in having a little chat."

"How did you know?" Richard was puzzled at the man's intuition.

"Because I was just like you only a little while ago. It's my guess that you stepped off the path in search of a rabbit. Am I right?"

Richard nodded, and his eyes lit up because it seemed that this man was about to reveal a profound secret. "You know what, you're right! I've been on a heck of a journey, and so far I've figured it out that I have to visualize what I want, and feel what it would be like to have it. The strangest things keep happening...I know that I want to be with my family, and each time I think about that, and feel the feelings that go with it, all the people around me just vanish."

"That's because you've set yourself apart from the masses. Most people wish for a rabbit, or say how nice it would be to get off the path, but only a rare few ever take the time to visualize doing it."

"How does visualizing help? Does it just sort of act as a mental rehearsal, so that I'm not so afraid to take the necessary steps?"

The man shook his head and grinned, as though he was about to share the most priceless secret of all. "Oh, no. It's so much more than that." The man paused, and Richard leaned in, baited and waiting for more. The man looked intently at Richard, and then seemed to change the subject. "What's your name?"

"Richard. Richard Goodman."

"Good to meet you. I'm Andrew, but you can call me Andy. Andy Zauff. You got anything to eat?"

"What? Um, yeah, I have part of a sandwich," Richard became guarded. "Why." He asked with inflection of obvious suspicion.

"Hmm. Oh never mind. I'm going to excuse myself to get some lunch. Maybe I'll see you around." The man politely tipped his head and turned away with a look in his eyes that said he was torturing poor Richard on purpose.

"Now wait a minute!" Richard was not about to let the man get away precisely at the moment he was to discover the secret.

The man turned around with a look of question in his face.

"Weren't you going to tell me how visualizing helps?"

"Well, yeah, perhaps. But it's lunchtime, and I intend to eat now." The man was frank, but kind.

"Okay, *fine*, if I give you the rest of my sandwich, will you stay and teach me what you know? Please?" Richard felt an urgency to seize the opportunity for knowledge even if doing so meant he had to abandon all pride. He didn't know if anyone else with this man's experience would ever bother to come along and give him the priceless knowledge that he so desperately sought.

Andy smiled and accepted the sandwich as Richard eagerly offered it in his outstretched hand. Granted, it was all that Richard owned. Would he ever be able to replace it? He thought of the men that fiercely competed for the one measly sack on the path, when so many others lay around, unnoticed. He knew there were other sacks, more so than some people realized. Trusting that the wisdom would be worth the price, he put away any concerns about being able to get another sandwich.

He'd simply go find one, expecting it to be there when he needed it.

The man ate Richard's food and motioned for him to sit down with him to continue their conversation.

"Contrary to what you may think, visualizing isn't just for generating courage." The man spoke very deliberately now, "Picturing a favorable circumstance in your head literally causes unseen things to happen in mysterious ways." He paused and searched Richard's face for signs of belief or skepticism. Seeing only wide-eyed curiosity, he proceeded. "Actually, some terribly misleading rumors are circulating among the paper sack collectors: they say that to leave the path one must have a *big enough dream* to do so. The problem is that the people think that means they need to have a big enough dream *to give them the motivation to do nearly super-human things.*" Richard was nodding, for that was a perspective he had encountered himself. "...But in actuality, it is the dream itself, the passionate thoughts of what they want, that emanate from their minds like radio waves and which go out into the universe, causing astonishing things to happen on their behalf."

The man's voice showed excitement, as if every time he thought about it, he was just as amazed as when he learned it for the first time. "In other words, if you get excited about holding a rabbit by the ears in your hands, rabbits will literally begin to approach you, merely by your thoughts. By thought they are drawn to you, by action you receive them."

"You're telling me that my thoughts make things happen that I can't see. I don't mean to be thick-headed here, but what are you *talking* about? What kind of thoughts?"

The man answered, "It's *so* incredibly simple! You've got to have *gratitude* for your present conditions, no matter what they are, because it is the lessons of the present that prepare you for the blessings of the future. Have grateful thoughts for your current situation. Also, you've got to have thoughts of how you'll feel when you reach your goal."

He added, "Thoughts of *trust* are vital, too; trust that a higher power is guiding you to find and catch your rabbit. And, most importantly, you must have thoughts of *belief* that there is a way, no matter what kind of obstacles may appear. These thoughts are all invisible but powerful little packages that go out and do for you many things that you can't do for yourself."

"So I have to be grateful even though I don't have a rabbit," Richard reiterated.

"Yes. Be genuinely grateful the way things are, and then be truly grateful for how things will be. You see, to be grateful for something before it

71

has been accomplished, is faith. And faith can move mountains."

"So, all those people who have rabbits just think differently than the rest of us? I thought they were just faster, stronger, or smarter."

"No, for the most part they're just like anyone else."

Richard wasn't quite convinced. Pointing toward a few of the folks in the distance who had rabbits he said, "But it comes so naturally to them. Every successful person I've ever known was self-confident. I've never seen them show any doubt. It's like they were born or raised that way. Me, on the other hand...I would really have to struggle to think that way consistently enough. It'd be so unnatural."

The rabbit man grinned and nodded his head understandingly. "Yes, it could take some practice. But truthfully, most of those people with rabbits had to develop the thought-discipline, too. Just like you." He chuckled, "You know, you're not the only one who has mistakenly deduced by observation that the winners are somehow more gifted than the rest. Isn't it ironic that the people *without* rabbits have all figured out what it takes to get one?"

Richard agreed, "Like the moron I saw who thought he'd catch a rabbit by jumping around like a dog."

"Oh you're kidding, right?"

"No, I'm not."

Andy rolled his eyes. "I wish people would just learn how to *think* differently. If they'd just learn how to *think* like a winner, they'd win! I'd tell them to *see* the rabbit vividly before launching a full-blown attack for crying out loud! I mean, that's just common sense! And I'd tell them: don't make excuses! Winners don't make excuses, period! Richard, in case you haven't noticed, excuses are epidemic out there on the path. Show me a person with an excuse and I'll show you a winner determined to succeed in spite of the same, or worse, circumstances. Nobody has an obstacle so great that there is not also a way prepared for that person to succeed. That's a promise."

He paused, as he searched Richard's face for understanding.

Richard spoke up, cautious not to sound like he was trying to make excuses, "Certainly there are times when a task is truly impossible, I mean, you'll never see a really old man place first in a triathlon, will you?"

With a slight grin, the man raised his eyebrows, blinked slowly, and shrugged his shoulders. "I've learned to never say 'never.' I've also learned that if I believe I can't do something under certain conditions, somewhere in the billions of people on this planet someone exists who would do it anyway. So I figure, why not me? And, if that was my dream, to win a triathlon as an old man, and if I could believe it, then it would be possible. But I'd need a pretty altruistic reason to do such a thing, and the desire would have to be intensely passionate. I'm sure that in the history of mankind, many old men have done impossibly physical tasks, equivalent to a triathlon, perhaps because their life depended on it. Miracles do happen."

"I just don't understand how a person can do something remarkable if they don't *already* have what it takes."

"I'll be honest; most people *can't* achieve their dreams...as they are. But people can change. Success comes when a person submits to change, but it isn't the kind of change that you'd suspect. See, although a person might not have all he needs to make something happen immediately, he certainly has all he needs to get started, and that's all that matters. If they picture themselves successful, and feel the victory as though it were real, and believe that somehow there will be a way, then they can expect it. They *must* expect it. Then when they go as far as they can go, and reach what appears to be a road-block, *that* is where they must expect to find the way around it."

Finally, Richard got it. He nodded, but now he wanted some specific advice about his own personal state of affairs. "Okay, with that said, all I want is to provide for my family, and spend my days enjoying their company. I don't want to spend my whole life in the sack-race."

"Do you know how you're going to do that?"

"I have no idea. But I believe that catching a rabbit will help."

"Okay, then. It's simple. You'll need to write it down, and *know* that the mere act of doing so causes unseen things to happen for your benefit."

"I need to write it down? What good does that do?"

"Well, it's funny. Visualization alone accomplishes a great many things. But it is a beautiful thing to commit a goal to paper and know that writing it down is just like submitting a request to the Master Chef. Since there's no waitress here, you have to put in your *own* order. When the dream comes just as you ordered, you can know for certain that the Master provided it. And He loves the recognition! When you only imagine it, and it comes true, there's the question of whether or not it was just a strange coincidence."

"You've got to be kidding. You mean, you write down what you want, and it comes?"

"Basically, yes. But there is more to it than that."

"Like what?" Richard's curiosity was piqued.

"Well, let me ask you something. If I were to go back to the path and tell everyone that all they needed to do was take the time to write down exactly what they wanted and it would come true, what do you think they would say?"

Richard chuckled. "I know what one of them would say, at least. He would tell you how annoying you are."

Andy laughed. "Yeah, I've heard that one. What do you think they would do if you told them to write down what they want?"

"Well, I doubt they would do anything. And even if they did write it down, I doubt they'd believe it would work."

"You're right. In fact, only approximately three percent of the population take it seriously. And, it's no surprise that only about three percent are able to get rabbits to come to them."

"No kidding."

"No, I'm not. See, the whole key is belief. People are used to believing only in what they can see, or detect with their senses. The three percent consciously choose to believe in something they create in their own mind. You are not presently with your family. But each time you close your eyes to imagine and feel that happy reunion, circumstances are literally changing, rabbits are actually approaching. Do that often enough, believing with no reservations that it is already true, and it *will happen*. By law."

"Law?!"

"Laws of thought."

"There are laws of thought? What in the world does that mean?" Richard's brows were furrowed and his eyes were wide.

"Well, just like gravity is a law of nature, so are there laws related to how our thoughts affect our circumstances. And, like gravity, we don't have to understand it or believe in it to be affected by it one hundred percent."

"You mean I've been governed by 'laws of thought' my whole life and never even knew it?"

"Exactly. Not very many people have discovered that their own thoughts significantly affect their circumstances. But those that have discovered it have found that the knowledge can be a great advantage to them. As they believe on purpose, the things they need are drawn to them. But when they let themselves doubt, the things are drawn away from them. This is how it works with absolutely everybody, but what do you think the problem is? Why don't you think it's obvious to everyone?" Andy wanted Richard to draw the conclusion himself.

"Well," Richard thought, "We think hundreds of things every day and never see evidence of them having any effect on anything."

"But they do. They really, really do."

Richard thought silently for a time. Finally he said, "I suppose our circumstances seem random because we don't hold on to one thought long enough to see it happen. We talk ourselves out of ideas. We believe, then we doubt, we believe, then we doubt, right?"

Andy replied, "You got it. It's like a cosmic dance...all that we could ever need is all around us. There is plenty for everyone, and if it ever ran out, more would be created. As we believe it's coming to us, it does. When we believe that we lack, it is drawn back. The dance: one step forward, it's on its way. One step back and it steps back as well."

"So...disbelief is the norm because all of this is happening in an invisible way. We never see the dance, so we have no idea that we are having any effect on it." Richard was energized. This knowledge was giving him a confidence that he never had before.

Andy could see the lights going on in Richard's eyes and he smiled. "Think of it this way: a tree seed that gets planted in the earth does not have to scramble around searching for bark particles, or leaf molecules, does it? Does it worry that it might not find what it needs?"

Richard chuckled, "Of course not."

"You're right. We can learn a lot from God through his creations in nature. No, the seed doesn't even have to look very far. It just remains still, and all that it needs is naturally drawn to it. In God's words, 'be still, and know that I am.'"

Remembering something he had been taught as a child, Richard added, "Consider the lilies of the field, how they grow...they toil not...but never was a king arrayed...quite as well as one of these?"

Andy simply smiled.

"I butchered that one, didn't I? I don't remember exactly how it goes."

"You get the idea, though." He continued, "If we think of our idea like a seed, and plant it in our minds, and nourish it with belief and gratitude, then all that we need to accomplish the idea is drawn to us just as naturally as elements to the lilies."

"Pshh. That makes so much sense."

"I love to see people finally get it. I used to try to tell everyone on the path how simple it was to have all of their needs met. But they were suspicious and talked illogically."

"How do you mean?" Richard was curious.

"Oh, I'd tell them they could go home to their family if they caught a rabbit, and they'd say they would if they had one, but since they didn't, they were trapped on the path. I'd tell them they could catch a rabbit if they learned how, and they'd say that they knew someone who had tried it before and failed. I'd tell them there's a better way, and they'd say they'd heard it all before. I got weary of trying to explain it. Ironic, isn't it?"

"Wow. I guess someone has to really want it before the answer will do them any good, huh?"

"That's what I've learned. Usually I just stop trying if they give me an excuse, two or three times in a row. No reason to waste the answers on someone who isn't asking the questions. It's like being a store clerk and handing a bathroom key to each and every customer who comes along and saying, 'Here, the restroom is down the second aisle, and then turn left. It will be at the end of the hall. Here, take the key. Take it! What do you mean you don't need it? Who wouldn't want to use the bathroom?!'" Andy held a pretend key in one hand and shook it in front of Richard's face while Richard swatted at it with his hand like it was a fly.

Andy continued, "I've learned it's a timing thing. The information simply isn't useful to everyone who comes along. Some come in for a soda or a newspaper, with no intentions of using a restroom. And in fact, when someone comes along who wants the restroom key, you *certainly* don't have to talk them into taking it! After all, only a relatively small number of people are looking for what you have. And you know what? That's okay."

Thinking about the hordes of people crowding the path, Richard suggested, "It's *my* guess there's a lot more than just three percent who want a rabbit, wouldn't you agree?"

"Yeah, I do. But not *that* many think they've got to change the way they think before they'll ever get one. Too many of them *wish* for a rabbit, hoping one might come their way out of sheer luck." Andy grinned. Suddenly he had an idea. "Follow me. I want to show you something."

Richard and Andy hurried to catch up with a few people who were walking along with rabbits in their hands. The man conferred with a few of them secretly for a moment, and one of them threw his head back in laughter. Each of them smiled in turn, and then they all nodded their heads. Andy turned again to Richard and said, "I'd like you to meet some of my friends: Colin O'Hare, Evan Yukon, and Cary Moore. Guys, this is Richard Goodman. Now, let's take a little trip back to the path. You've gotta see this."

Returning to the old road, Richard glanced over his shoulder and politely nodded his head to the three strangers, extremely curious about what was going to happen next.

The dream itself, the passionate thoughts
of what I want, will emanate from my mind
like radio waves and will go out
into the universe, causing astonishing things
to happen on my behalf!

There is no obstacle so great that
there is not also a way prepared
for me to succeed!

I have all I need to get started,
and that's all that matters.

I will write it down.
I will 'submit' my goal
to the Master Chef.

~ CHAPTER NINE ~
THE GIVEAWAY

Andy Zauff turned to Richard and said, "Do you want to see why our thinking has everything to do with the degree of success we enjoy?"

Intrigued, Richard glanced at the three others who stood near him, smiling. They obviously couldn't wait to witness Richard's reaction.

Without another word, Andy gathered up all of the rabbits from the group and held them securely in both hands. He had five rabbits. The other participants in this scheme made themselves comfortable on the ground next to each other, facing the path. If there had been bleachers, Richard was sure by the eager look on their faces they would have been on the front row, with hot dogs and soda in hand. With uncertainty, Richard chose to sit beside them.

Andy asked Richard, "Which one of those people on the path do you think would like some rabbits today?"

Richard's eyes grew wide, "What? What are you going to do?!"

"Just pick someone."

"Um, okay…How about that guy?" Richard pointed to a very average looking fellow, wearing khaki pants and a polo shirt with a "too cool for you" strut.

"Fine. Now watch this…" Andy took the rabbits, and walking away from his friends, he stepped onto the path directly in front of the khaki pants man. "Excuse me, a minute; I have something to give you."

"Out of my way, punk." The khaki pants man pushed the Andy aside and walked on.

Turning to Richard, Andy hollered, "Pick someone else!"

Richard pointed to a thin man in a suit and glasses.

Andy stepped in front of the thin man. "Excuse me, sir; I have something to give you."

The thin man stopped and eyed the rabbit man suspiciously and said, "What?" There was no modulation in his voice whatsoever.

"You are the lucky recipient today of five, fine rabbits."

"What's it going to cost me?" The thin man's voice remained monotone and somewhat irritated.

"Nothing, whatsoever. No strings attached, I'm just conducting an experiment."

"No thanks," the thin man put up his hand and hurried away.

Looking back at the crew who sat at the side of the path, Andy raised his shoulders as if seeking further input.

Richard held out his hands, palms up, as if to say, "You choose."

So Andy stood in the path and called out, "Free rabbits, five-fine-free rabbits!" But people just looked at him oddly and walked past.

Finally he hollered, "Today's jackpot is FIVE FINE RABBITS! Who's got a lottery ticket!?"

With that, quite a few people frantically searched their pockets and approached him, shaking their tickets and chattering excitedly.

Looking back at his comrades, Andy saw they were doubled over in laughter. Richard was stunned.

Andy arbitrarily snatched someone's ticket and said, "You're the lucky one!" Then he put all ten rabbit ears into one hand, and offered them to the jumping, screaming winner.

The winner awkwardly took hold of the ten rabbit ears and panted excitedly. The others on the path had mixed reactions. Some cheered him and stayed close, offering to help and declaring their lifelong friendship, while others cussed and grumbled and stormed away.

Returning to his friends empty handed, Andy parked himself on the ground, obviously not finished with his investigation. Richard was amazed that these rabbit people would sacrifice such a valuable commodity for the sake of an experiment on his behalf.

Somewhere in the cloud of dust, the winner was surrounded by the crowds of people who had gathered. Quite a commotion ensued, and even cameras flashed from reporters who had been drawn to the scene and couldn't wait to get their story on the front page of the morning paper.

Then out from under the throngs of people scampered a rabbit that had escaped the madness. Hopping off the path and into the grass, it actually approached Colin and stopped directly in front of him. Colin reached out and took hold of the rabbit, and the others patted him on the back.

One by one, the rabbits returned, and Richard was utterly speechless. Once all of the rabbits were back, Richard looked toward the path and saw that the crowd had dispersed. The only one left was the 'winner,' moping empty handed and searching for a paper sack.

It was a depressing sight. Richard didn't like the way this scene made him feel. Sensing Richard's concern, Andy nodded, "I know how you're feeling. Believe me, this is the most frustrating part about owning a heightened awareness of the laws. It's painful to see how blind others can be, especially when it doesn't have to be that way. That man can have all the rabbits he wants, but he has to change the way he thinks. Some people have to hit rock bottom before they're humble enough to start asking the right questions."

"Couldn't we just teach him how to think? Help him succeed?"

"Believe me; I've tried with many a sack collector and even a few rabbit owners who got their rabbits in cut-throat ways. But most people just aren't interested in what I have to say, and those who *are* interested tend not to believe me. Only people who want the knowledge desperately enough seem to listen to me *and* apply what I teach. They have to want the knowledge at least as much as they want food."

It all came together for Richard now. "The sandwich. You had to find out how badly I wanted this knowledge, didn't you? You probably weren't even hungry, were you?"

"Well, actually I was. But you're right. I had to know if you were going to waste my time or not, and if you were going to waste your *own* time or not. Without considerable sacrifice, people just don't seem to follow through. That's why I started asking for sandwiches. Some people see it as greedy, but in reality I'm doing them a favor." The three comrades stood, and Andy shook their hands from his sitting position and said, "Thank you for your help."

They each smiled and said, "My pleasure," or, "No problem."

Richard spoke slowly, as if to himself, "Greedy? Greedy to ask for a sandwich so that he can change someone's life?" Richard wasn't sure *what* he thought about that.

Having overheard Richard's mumbling, Andy said, "It's as though I have plenty of water, fertilizer, and sunshine that I'll gladly pour out on anyone's ground. But if they are so tight-fisted that they won't put their measly seed in the soil, all that I have to offer will be wasted."

"Okay, I've heard something like that before: What you send out comes back to you...or that which ye reap, so shall ye sow... Is that what this is all about?"

"Yep, but you have to be careful with that cliché. Too many people try to apply that principle improperly, and the money *never* comes back to them. Then they wonder why it didn't work, and lose faith that it is a valid promise. There's a fine line between a sacrifice or investment, and gambling. Make sure you know the difference."

"So, I suppose an investment in knowledge that empowers me somehow is a true investment, while a lottery ticket is gambling?"

"Yes, that is the one of the more obvious distinctions...Still, there are less obvious forms of gambling, too."

Richard leaned back on his elbows and waited for the explanation.

Andy continued, "Have you ever made a huge sacrifice for some kind of venture based solely on someone's recommendation; maybe an advertisement, or a well-meaning friend or relative?"

"Oh boy, more times than I'd like to admit." Richard threw his head back and grimaced.

"What were you sacrificing for?"

"What do you mean?"

"I mean, specifically, why did you make the sacrifice? What did you expect to *get out of it*? What specific things were you going to *do* with the profits? How was it going to *feel* to enjoy those profits? About how long did you think you'd have to wait before you'd be able to *harvest* the profits?" Andy was leaning forward, throwing the questions at Richard in rapid fire, with an obvious tone of accusation. He knew full well that Richard had not taken the time to think through these details before making the so-called investment.

Richard was feeling somewhat cornered. Sheepishly, he responded, "Oh, heck. I didn't think too much about any of that. I just trusted that the people knew what they were talking about and that each of the ventures promised to make me a bunch of money. Their ideas honestly made a lot of sense to me!"

"That, my friend, was gambling. I don't doubt that the people probably knew what they were doing. I suspect they had those questions nailed down solid for themselves, and they probably *did* make a ton of money. But you're the one who didn't see your own rabbit, and you're the fool who jumped, barked, and chased nothing but air."

Richard sighed. This awareness was depressing him, actually. Trying to divert such uncomfortable focus on his past foolishness, he changed the subject back to his most recent *smart* investment. "Well, in case you were concerned about the sandwich thing, I'm really not put out by that. I'd do it again if I had to. You've taught me how to fish, for Pete's sake, and you can't put a price tag on that. Half of a sandwich? Pshh! What a bargain."

Andy kindly consented to the diversion. "That's right; you *have* come a long way. Forgive my attack on your past decisions; I just wanted to emphasize the importance of having your own dreams and goals vividly defined before taking action in an investment or business venture. With your dream securely in place, you will be steered by a higher power toward the right decisions for *you*."

"Hey, I'm okay with that. I've just experienced a little growing pain to face the fact that I haven't been all that wise about those kinds of things."

"But you're on your way now, and that's what matters."

"I'm on my way now. That's right." Richard stood up and extended his hand. "Well I am awfully grateful, and can hardly wait to get started..."

"Remember: Whatever you need to accomplish your goal will be drawn to you once you have planted the seed in your mind. Plant it, get emotional about it, be grateful for it, and KNOW that all things that you will need are literally approaching. Just like the elements to the tree seed." He smiled, "Now, my fine friend, I am really happy to know you, and I wish you the best. I'm going now to have my own dream fulfilled: my family is waiting for my arrival as we speak." With a smile, he saluted Richard and held up the rabbit in a gesture meaning goodbye.

Richard smiled and saluted him back. "Thank you and God bless!"

Whatever I need to accomplish my goal will be drawn to me once I have planted the seed in my mind.

~ CHAPTER TEN ~
THE CATCH

Richard couldn't seem to wipe the grin off of his face. He knew, *he knew*, that it was actually in *his own* control to achieve his goal. No longer did his success depend upon whether a rabbit *happened* to come along. He didn't need to *hope* the circumstances would be in his favor. He didn't need to worry if he would be fast enough or smart enough or better than the next guy. Success was completely within his control! Competition was unnecessary because enough rabbits abounded for everyone! And if the rabbits ever ran out, more would be created. God had provided, and would continue to provide plenty to all who believed in abundance.

In fact, he was getting hungry, so he returned briefly to the path to get himself another sack with a sandwich and realized with gratitude that God even provides an abundance of sacks on the path. He deduced if every person without a sack truly believed they would find one, and if there literally was *not* enough to go around, more would be created, by God's law.

Believing in plenty made it possible for Richard to always see more. He remembered the blonde competitor and wished he could have given *him* a shot of belief, because the act of willful belief would have actually opened his eyes to what had been all around him the whole time.

Richard laughed joyfully out loud, "I think I believe in abundance! There is no such thing as lack! There is only abundance!" He was energized. He had felt so hopeless for so long, that having this new awareness caused him to drop to his knees, arms spread with his face to the sky, overcome with gratitude because he knew how to provide for his family, no matter what the circumstances. He realized, *no matter what the circumstances are I can always choose my own thoughts.* These new ideas were utterly astonishing to him. He sat back on his heels and took a moment to enjoy the entire sandwich one grateful bite at a time.

While still on his knees, his heart swelled with the feeling of gratitude and he envisioned with his eyes closed the rabbit he hoped to capture. *Dear God, will you please grant me a rabbit?* This time, he put in the extra effort to add detail in his mind. He made the rabbit well-defined, and it was beautiful, with long, graceful ears and suede-like fur. He could see every detail of the creature, right down to the tiny white fuzz on the edges of its ears, and the strong, sloping back and puffy white tail.

Finally, he expressed gratitude for it as though it was already his. "Thank you for this wonderful rabbit I now have!"

He opened his eyes slowly, but nothing was there. *It didn't work. I did what he said, and there's no rabbit here.* Richard felt a twinge of disappointment but consciously applied the proper laws of thought which he had just learned. He closed his eyes again and thought, *It's already mine, and I know that as I* choose *to believe, it is actually approaching. God, help me know what to do and where to go so that I can do my part.*

Richard opened his eyes and still did not see a rabbit, but he smiled anyway, because he knew it was only a matter of time, so long as he continued to believe.

Okay, God, tell me what to do. I'm really ready to follow your instructions. Richard truly expected to hear something, perhaps a booming voice from the clouds, or an angelic, musical whisper in his ear. But he heard nothing. Maybe the inspiration would come as words to his mind. But since he perceived no communication from Deity, he decided to just get up and start walking. After all, he knew for a fact that you can't steer a parked car.

As he walked, a thought did come to him that his idea to simply start walking could very well have been the inspiration he was looking for.

It was a strange thought, because he had expected something much more dramatic to get his attention. Rather, he chose to trust in the imperceptible guidance. He gave God the credit for getting him up off the stump. It just felt right to do so. And now that he had shifted himself into first gear, he trusted that God had the steering wheel. His job was to roll, God's job was to steer.

The grass was especially tall now where he walked, and he pushed it out of his way with each step. Before long, he pushed aside another thick wave of grass and there in front of him sat the most beautiful rabbit he had ever seen. Just as he had imagined, the long ears were graceful and looked like the finest grey brown suede. He noticed the color inside of the ears was soft and white. Tiny white fuzz lined the rims and even glowed in the lowering sun. The rabbit breathed slowly. There was no hint that it was wary. Richard's eyes followed the hunch of the rabbit's back as it sloped to a beautiful white tail. He looked into its eyes and it held Richard's gaze. It was as though it was challenging him to succeed. How uncanny it seemed that it had just barely come out of the hole where it hid, only inches away.

Amazed, Richard did not restrain his excitement and lurched forward, startling the rabbit. Did he see disappointment in the hare's eyes? It seemed as if the rabbit was saying, "You want it to be harder than it has to be? All right, I'll make it harder..."

It darted away and Richard ran after it. Diving for it, he caught hold of its foot but it was trying to scamper so fiercely that he lost his grip, and rolling over he leapt again to try to grab it. It was quick, and he missed. The rabbit didn't seem frantic, but rather like it was goading him. Richard had a fleeting thought that he didn't deserve this fine rabbit, but giving up at this point was not an option. He jumped and darted, chasing it hard, and finally he had it by its ears.

Panting, he stood up and turned to hear a faint chattering. He saw a woman near the path, actually with one foot on and one foot off, whispering to the child on her back that the man looked insane and they'd better hurry on.

Richard grinned, realizing she hadn't been able to see the object of his pursuit, and held up the rabbit to show her why the madness.

Shaking her head, she rolled her eyes and patted her babe's hand, and resolutely returned to the path. "Showoff," he heard her say.

Richard felt sad. He also felt like he was out of breath. *That was a serious workout! I couldn't take too much more of that. But at least I got him! I got him! Felicity, I'm coming home!*

~~~~~

In the forest, the snake spotted a squirrel. It turned, then quietly slithered off Richard's chest and wrapped itself around the trunk of the tree, creeping upward in pursuit.

Whatever my circumstances are,
I can always choose my own thoughts.

~ CHAPTER ELEVEN ~
THE CHOICE

The officer questioning Felicity was not about to waste any more time. If she had something to say, she evidently wasn't going to say it in the next ten minutes, and he was becoming bored. Finally, he stated calmly, "Ma'am, I'm leaving. You think about what I told you, and let's hope he turns up...for his sake as well as your own."

Just at that moment his radio bleeped on with a coded message and a chirp. "Oh— see, I've got to go, but you let us know if you decide to start talking again, alright?" And with that, he quickly gathered his things in a haphazard bundle, stuffed them into his briefcase and closed the latches. He could have said, "Lady, you are a freak," and it wouldn't have been any clearer than the condescending body language he displayed.

The worry in Felicity's eyes deepened, and the feeling of hopelessness filled every last part of her. The officer stood, causing the aluminum-legged chair to squeak as he pushed it backwards on the aged linoleum. He automatically and without intent tipped his hat, motioned for his partner to come along, pushed the screen door open wide so it banged hard behind them, and they were gone.

Felicity was stunned. "They aren't going to do anything. They think *I've* done something..." Her anxiety suddenly mounted and she cried angrily, "He could be dead RIGHT NOW and they aren't doing ANYTHING about it!!!" With her foot, she shoved the chair that was still tipped over and it hit the wall with a bang.

Matthew came out of his room rubbing his sleepy eyes. "Mommy? What was that?" He stopped and looked at his mother. He stepped back into the bedroom when he saw she had black around her eyes, white in the corners of her mouth, curled tendrils plastered to her forehead, and streaks on her cheeks.

Not knowing what to think, his lower lip pouted out and his eyes turned glassy. Felicity could see he was about to cry. She opened her arms and he reluctantly approached her. She hugged the little boy and broke down. "Oh, honey, I'm sorry. I sort of kicked the chair; I didn't mean to wake you up." Felicity forced the words because she had so convinced herself that something was wrong that she struggled to provide him any comfort. What she needed was someone to hold *her* close and offer *her* reassuring words.

But nobody would. Nobody could. Nobody knew.

"I wanna see Daddy now," Matthew whined.

"But he's not home yet, sweetie."

"How come?"

Felicity opened her mouth to answer, but couldn't think of what to say.

"What's wrong, Mom? I'm scared."

Looking into Matthew's concerned face, she surrendered inside. She knew deep down that all she imagined had been without real evidence, and it wasn't fair to take her little four year-old on this imaginary panic trip. Part of her still worried, but she forced herself to hope. It wasn't the natural way to think. It wasn't the easy way to think. But she *had* to imagine that Richard was well and that they would see him again. She glanced down at her palms and realized that her own thoughts, her own imaginations had caused them to get very moist. She looked through the door into her bedroom mirror and saw her face, makeup smeared and cheeks tear-stained. Finally, she saw the dried icing in the corners of her mouth, and the cracker glob on her shirt. She appeared deranged. No wonder the officers had treated her the way they did.

She looked again at Matthew and with new resolve she knelt down in front of him and held his arms. Gazing directly into his reddened eyes, she said tenderly, "Matthew, everything is fine. Daddy is just fine," Felicity's voice cracked, "and we're going to go see him now. You understand?"

Matthew's face softened and he said, "Okay." He placed his arms around his mother and sniffled.

"Let's go. We'll find him before it gets dark."

Felicity took a deep breath and stepped into the bathroom to spot clean her shirt and wash her face, patting it dry with the terrycloth hand towel and then hanging the towel neatly on the rack. Finally, it was also time to pick up the fallen chair and place it neatly next to the others at the table. She gently pushed it in and then touched it once more affectionately, feeling new resolve. Felicity realized she felt better. She truly didn't feel so worried, just hearing her own voice speak words of faith. *What if you're wrong?* A little voice inside her head taunted her. She spoke to herself, "When I have a choice, *I choose to believe.*" Merely believing couldn't be any more harmful than the damage she may have already done, worrying Matthew so.

What if she *was* wrong? She'd cross that bridge when she came to it. All she had was now, and all she would allow herself to do was believe.

When I have a choice,
I choose to believe.

~ CHAPTER TWELVE ~
VIOLATIONS

Richard was also on his way. He had left the path, and he had a rabbit. Looking toward the people on the path, he felt a compelling urge to help them learn what he had learned. He had a rabbit! Anyone could have a rabbit, truly! He couldn't contain himself; he wanted to show them what could be theirs. He held up his rabbit and waved, just to see if anyone would stop and talk to him. Wouldn't anyone come ask him how to do it? He showed them that he knew how, why didn't they want to know for themselves?

But deep down he knew what they were saying to each other. *"Look at the guy... thinking he's so much better than us."* Or, *"Oh, what an unfortunate man; destined to lose his soul over a lust for rabbits."*

He could also detect their thoughts: *"Yeah, a rabbit would be nice. Maybe someday a rabbit will fall into the path right in front of me, too."* Or, *"I knew I should have gone to school to learn rabbit anatomy so I could catch rabbits just like him."*

Additionally, there were the folks who were very close to stepping off the path, but were paralyzed by the same fears he had experienced: fearing risk, fearing answers, fearing abundance, fearing success. *"What if I lose my way without a path? What if I don't know how to handle a rabbit? What if I catch one and it gets away, and then I can't ever find another paper sack? What if I catch one that snatches the only sandwich I have and runs away? What if people laugh at me? What if I fail?"*

Taking one more look at the crowd, Richard had to simply carry on. He was breaking new ground, charting his own course. He looked ahead at the meadow that lay between the path and the woods, and he pressed forward.

He seemed to travel for hours, retracing his steps, almost. This time he walked in the less traveled area off the road. Along the way he came to meet many a man and woman with a rabbit in their clutches. In fact, he had never realized how many people had discovered the secret, but now that he knew it, he saw them everywhere. With a heightened awareness, he realized they must have been there all along.

He gazed admiringly at the people who seemed to be strolling home, so happy and accomplished. But his feel-good warm and fuzzy emotions were interrupted by two men who seemed to have arrived out of nowhere and were whispering emphatically at one another. Richard

108

turned to see who they were, and saw that the men were clawing each other's shirt sleeves, teeth gritted, whispering angry words that Richard couldn't quite decipher.

Finally one of the men thrust his hands off of the other man's shirt, and bending down into the grass as best as he could, he clamored to get ahead of the other man as they both seemed to be pursuing a rabbit.

Splitting up, they attempted to surround the creature, and the faster one leapt ahead with a full-body attack, trying to pin it down once and for all. The other man wearing a camouflage jacket pounced on top of the first, and the yelling began. Richard could not determine the fate of the rabbit, but he heard the scuffle and watched them fighting each other viciously in an attempt to win the prize. Eventually he heard a loud thud and a groan, and the second man in the jacket stood, triumphantly gripping the hare in his fist. A forceful nudge with his foot to the fallen man, and he walked away, limping and gloating gracelessly in his victory.

Richard rushed over to help the fallen man get back on his feet. The man lay there groaning, but when he slapped the ground angrily with one of his hands, Richard could see that his pain was that of wounded pride, more than that of any physical injury.

"I'm fine, I'm fine."

"Are you sure? Who was that guy?" Richard was genuinely concerned.

"Oh, he's just my best friend, or should I say, my *ex-* best friend. First class creep." The man brushed off his pant legs and struggled to his feet. "He and I decided to go rabbit hunting together...we were sick of the sack-race and decided to do it big by getting ourselves a rabbit. We finally found one, and when he got really irritable I realized he wasn't really planning on sharing the spoils. You saw the rest."

Richard brushed some loose grass off of the back of the man's flannel shirt. Bowing his head the man held up his hand casually, and said, "Thanks for the hand, uh...."

"Richard. The name's Richard Goodman."

"Gavin. Gavin Upnow. Thanks again," he replied then limped away.

Gavin Upnow? You've gotta be kidding. Richard mused at the collection of characters he had met along this journey. At every turn he seemed to be presented with intriguing, perplexing, confusing, enlightening, and even mind-bending encounters.

Richard looked over at a few of the rabbit people and the evidence of their 'success' as they walked and wondered how many of them had captured their rabbits by living in harmony with God's natural laws of thought, and how many had actually contended for it. *I think I'd rather do it God's way. It's hard enough catching one of the little thumpers without having some other guy pounding you into the ground at the same time.*

As Richard continued to reflect, one more question kept gnawing at him. How is it possible that some of the people held in their hands two, three, and up to six rabbits by the ears? He knew how hard it had been to catch one, even without competing for it; how did some of these people have so many in their fists? Dozens of people of all kinds held multiple rabbits: short, tall, heavy, thin, men, women...even an occasional adolescent. It seemed that all kinds of people had managed to catch several rabbits. He would have expected only the most athletic and agile to have been able to chase and wrestle a rabbit down with one or more already in their fist.

He made eye contact with one of the shorter, heavier ones. He was a pleasant looking, clean shaven young man in his forties, with a large round belly and twinkle in his eye. He wore a snugly fitted hunter-green polo shirt with a shiny black belt that disappeared under his gut and baggy, off white trousers. His shoes were glossy slip-ons with leather tassels. The man looked at Richard's rabbit and grinned. With a knowing twitch of his head, the man beckoned Richard to walk alongside him for a while.

Richard of course didn't need further encouragement. "The student was ready" and he was eager to learn what this man knew. The man obviously had not wrangled the four rabbits he held. That would have been physically impossible. Besides, his clothes showed no sign of dirt or grass stains like Richard had on his own clothing.

"I know what you're thinking, because I was just like you only a short while ago," the man said when Richard caught up to him.

Richard looked again at the abundance of rabbits in this man's grasp. "Oh really?" He enjoyed the mystic aura that emanated from these people who knew so much, and he thought it interesting that the more he learned, the less mystic, or mysterious all of it really was.

A bird sailed by overhead and he looked up. It made him consider the laws of aerodynamics, and how scary it would have been for people to see humans put them to use centuries before they had been discovered. Imagine the alarm that his forebears might have felt, had they seen a 747 airliner soar over their heads. Oh how mystic *that* would have seemed!

Just like the laws of aerodynamics, he realized now that these laws of thought had always existed, too. But he didn't understand them before now, or know how to use them to his advantage. He remembered being taught all his life to "doubt not," "fear not,"...and now he was finally beginning to understand why. *It just simply isn't good for me! The things I want and need are repelled, literally, when I allow myself to entertain the negative emotions of doubt and fear.*

He recalled several times when he had allowed himself to think about things he *didn't* want. *What if that tornado on the horizon is going to come rip my house apart?* He was eight years old and he remembered actually visualizing the destruction, feeling the horror as though it was already happening. It then began to come his way, and out of sheer terror he rushed down into the cellar and closed his eyes and ears, and then forced himself to picture the house standing strong and unaffected in sunny, peaceful weather. After all, it was the only thought which brought him peace...to pretend things were just the way he wanted them to be. He wanted to escape the storm's wrath, and the only way he could was in his own mind. He tuned it all out to live completely in his fantasy...

...and the house remained.

Richard thought back on that experience in awe. Had he actually had any influence whatsoever on the elements? He wasn't sure. He remembered other experiences when he had imagined something that didn't come true, and he deduced that it was probably because he didn't want it bad enough, or long enough, or believe innocently enough. Or maybe it just wasn't an appropriate desire, and he expressed gratitude for a God who still knew what was best for him.

But as for providing for his family, and being with them, nothing but peace came as he thought about that. To him, that meant that it was a commendable aspiration, and that God would help him achieve it, as long as he did not violate the laws of thought.

Finally, the short, heavy man in the green polo shirt derailed Richard's train of thought. "Really," he said. "I know what you're thinking because I was just like you only a short while ago. I, myself only had one rabbit, and I had worked up quite a sweat to obtain it. So now, you want to know how to catch more than one rabbit, because that first one was quite a doozy, right?"

"Oh, yeah." Richard was able to sense somehow that this man was living in harmony with God's laws. Maybe it was a glow, or energy that he was subconsciously picking up. He couldn't understand how he sensed it, but he did nonetheless. The feeling was just as identifiable as the times when he would walk into a room and know instantly that Felicity was in a cheerful mood, even if he couldn't see her face.

The man's eyes twinkled, for here was someone whose mind was open and who was eager to hear more. "What's your name?"

114

Richard responded with his full name, Richard A. Goodman.

Then the man remarked, "Well, Richard, I am guessing you discovered that to visualize the rabbit in detail brought it to you."

"Right," Richard replied.

"Would you believe me if I told you that the rest of my rabbits basically cocked their head to my hands and let me take their ears?"

"No. You can't be serious." Then Richard remembered the comrades and how the rabbits had returned to them effortlessly as well.

"I *am* serious. The first one is always the hardest. Let me guess, how you pictured it in your mind was kind of vague, wasn't it? And the rabbit was somewhat hard to see once you found it, am I right?"

Richard thought for a moment, and said, "You're right. You are absolutely right. I had a hard time seeing it in my mind, and when it appeared, it also was hard to see, and far away. In fact, that first one I couldn't catch at all. The next time, I visualized every detail I could imagine, and it appeared, just like I had seen it in my mind. But when I lunged at it, it ran away and I nearly wore myself right out capturing it. Still, I caught it, and here it is." Richard held up his furry loot. "I was just on my way home to share it with my family."

The man grinned. "Obtaining more rabbits is a piece of cake if you know what to do."

Richard still felt the urgency to get home, but he chose to sacrifice a little more time for what promised to be the education of a lifetime. A smirk crept over Richard's face and he had to know, "Is your name something like Ina Everett Thynn?"

"Huh?" The man looked at Richard like he was nuts.

"Oh, never mind. Okay, then, what do I do?"

"The name's Randy Mollup." He looked questioningly at Richard again and then continued, "So how badly *do* you want to know what I know?" The man was blunt and unapologetic.

Richard sighed, knowing full well what must inevitably happen next if he was serious about gaining this higher level of understanding. He thought for a moment, and then a latent streak of rebellion emerged. He responded challengingly, "I have no more sandwiches, Mr. Mollup."

The man shrugged and gave Richard a look of pity. "I am sorry for you, then. If you can't find a way to make the necessary sacrifice, then our conversation must end here."

Richard wised up. Attempting to meet the man on his own level, he said, "Now hang on just a minute..." Richard held up his hand as if to say "Wait here," and he closed his eyes. As quickly as he could, he created an image of the two men

116

conversing, and tried to feel the wonder he expected to feel when he learned the secret.

He knew he had done just that when the corners of his mouth automatically turned up. Upon opening his eyes, he confidently told the man, "I am going to learn what you know."

"Oh, are you?" The man was amused at Richard's under-developed comprehension and insolent remark. "And what makes you think I am going to share what I know?"

"Because I visualized it happening, and I felt it happen, so now I know it will."

"You provide me some compensation, and I will explain to you precisely why the conversation you visualized *won't* happen." With that, Mr. Mollup winked and strolled away.

Doubt not, fear not!
It just simply isn't good for me.

How badly do I want wisdom?

~ CHAPTER THIRTEEN ~
THE SACRIFICE

Richard stood there and his jaw hung open. *What did I do wrong?* His mind spun and he felt stupid for being so presumptuous, and unknowingly revealing his ignorance.

He could not let Mr. Mollup get too far away. *Quick! Think, Richard, think...how can I get him to talk to me?*

Just then the rabbit twitched in his hand. He looked down and his eyes widened. "Oh, no...he wouldn't expect me to— there's no way."

Richard looked up at the man, who was getting farther away with each passing moment. At the same time, the man turned his head and continuing to stroll along, he met Richard's gaze. The look in his eyes said, "C'mon, haven't you figured it out by now?"

Richard could scarcely believe what he was about to do. He closed his eyes once more, bracing himself for the painful decision he was about to make. Taking a deep breath, he held up the rabbit briefly and then began to trot ahead to catch up with Mr. Mollup.

Charitably, the man stopped and waited for him. As Richard approached, he was shaking his head repeatedly, venting his disbelief that he was actually going to give away the biggest bounty he had ever achieved for nothing but knowledge.

Closing his eyes again, he held out the rabbit for the man to take, and winced with anticipation for the torturous exchange.

"You sure you want to do this?" Mr. Mollup asked.

"Take it already! Take it!" Richard's eyes remained closed.

Mr. Mollup carefully opened his last two fingers on his left hand which already held his two other rabbits, and closed them again around the new rabbit's ears.

Richard finally opened his eyes and looked longingly at the rabbit. He felt queasy in the pit of his stomach, but pressed his lips together firmly, inhaled through his nose and said, "Okay?"

Nodding, the man complimented Richard. "That took some guts, my friend. I applaud your foresight. You'll be very glad that you did that, and with that kind of courage, you will very quickly recoup your investment...PLUS you'll have the knowledge you seek."

"I know I will. I fully expect to." Richard straightened up, as he felt a growing confidence in his decision.

"How quickly do you expect to get your rabbit back?"

"*My* rabbit?"

Mr. Mollup didn't say anything; he simply waited for Richard to respond.

Richard sensed he was being tested again, and he tried to interpret Mr. Mollup's body language and verbal clues. He was gun shy for having made a fool of himself only a few minutes before. But he had nothing more to lose except his pride, and he was realizing that the last wound to his pride hadn't been exactly fatal.

The good man raised his eyebrows and Richard, throwing up his hands let out all the stops, "I expect to get MY rabbit back before we're done talking today." Immediately he raised his cheeks and eyebrows, squinting.

There was a twinkle in Mr. Mollup's eye, and Richard felt a wave of relief. Perhaps he had said the right thing this time.

"What do you do when you want a raise at work, Richard?"

"I never got a raise at work."

"Why is that?"

"They just didn't give them out, except for the annual cost of living increase."

"How do you know they didn't give any out?"

"I don't know, I guess 'cause I never got one."

"Did you ever go into your boss' office and come right out and ASK for one?"

"No..."

"What about your bank account. Have you ever asked your bank to reverse a service charge, or overdraft fee?"

"No, I haven't. I didn't know you could."

Mr. Mollup stared Richard down and waited for the lights to go on in his head.

Finally they did. Richard's eyes grew large, and the man smiled. Richard held his gaze and turned his head slightly, communicating the question, "You mean...?"

The man responded with raised eyebrows, as if he expected Richard to make the next move.

Finally Richard spoke. "Will...you...give me my rabbit back?"

Mr. Mollup relaxed, and it was suddenly clear that he had been waiting for Richard to finally 'get it' this whole time. Handing the rabbit back to Richard, he said, "You'll get what you ask for out of life, Richard. Have the courage to ask. Have the guts to go after what you want. The worst that can happen is you'll hear 'no.' The best that can happen is you'll get what you want."

Richard was never as full of gratitude for that rabbit as he was then. He stroked it affectionately and then looking back up at Mr. Mollup, he asked, "Are you still going to teach me?"

122

The man didn't respond.

Richard pursed his lips together and then, as if a light went on in his head, he articulated, "Mr. Mollup, *will* you please teach me?"

"Yes, I will. But please call me Randy." Randy smiled and motioned for Richard to sit down on the grassy mound nearby.

It seemed so long ago, but Richard had not forgotten, "You said you would explain to me why, initially, you were *not* going to engage in a conversation with me, even though I visualized it *and* felt it."

Randy Mollup grinned and nodded. Leaning closer, he gazed intently into Richard's eyes. "Tell me this: why did you want to have that conversation so badly?"

"Because I knew it would help me get a ton of rabbits."

"Then why didn't you just go ahead and visualize a handful of rabbits, instead of visualizing the two of us having a conversation?"

"What difference would that have made?"

"Two things. Number one, you have no right to manipulate *my* own free agency by the thoughts you choose. Never try to visualize people doing things for you. You visualize the *outcome*, and the right people will do the right things to help it happen. But you do not know who the right people are, so you cannot decide that part. That isn't your place.

"Number two: if you had visualized the ultimate *reason* for wanting my knowledge, then you would have *instinctively* known what your next move should be. In this case, your move would have been to provide me with compensation, no matter what the cost."

Richard bit his lip and nodded, as the realization of his mistake sunk in. "Okay, I see what you mean."

"Let's move on. You wanted to know how to catch multiple rabbits, right?"

"That's right. That's why I'm here."

"Well let's go back to the time when you spotted your first rabbit. Now, you said that you saw it sort of vague in your mind, and then it was far away and hard to see when it appeared."

"Yes, that's right. And it ran away before I could do anything about it."

"And what about the first one you *caught*? It's my guess that you saw it pretty vividly in your mind, but it still wasn't easy to catch."

"Yeah, you're right...I saw it very vividly, and when it appeared, it was right there, in front of me, just as I had pictured it. But I had to chase it, and it *almost* got away from me."

"Well, if you want a rabbit to come to *you*, then you've got to take the time to visualize the rabbit *already in your hands.* And you have to feel the fur in your mind. And sense its warmth as you hold it in your fingers. Make it vivid. And even better still, you visualize a look in its eyes that it is entirely pleased to serve you, and be with you, because you treat it with respect."

"But aren't you going to end up eating it?"

"Not necessarily, we'll actually care for it and let it breed, so we will have an unlimited supply. Some will be eaten, but even those are happy to serve because they are God's creation, created to provide the needs of other creatures."

"So that's why my first rabbit was tough, because I had in mind an expectation that it didn't want to be with me? That it would be hard to get, and so it was?"

"You got it."

"So if I want a rabbit, do I imagine one *coming* to me, and then picture myself *grasping* it? Is that how I make it happen?"

"*No.* You aren't going to *make* anything happen. Too many people mess it all up with that mentality. Instead, imagine it already with you. See, don't be like the people who spend all kinds of wasted time visualizing circumstances *moving toward* their favor, trying to 'make things happen'. Instead, experience the feelings of success as though it has *already* been accomplished. Allowing yourself to *experience* it sort of puts you in a state of being that is in harmony, so to speak, with the thing you want. Then the right people and things will *naturally* be attracted to you, and do what needs to be done, because it gets *them* what they want as well. The fact of the matter is that using our minds to try to force things or people to do stuff is in violation of basic universal law. "

"Like I tried to do with you."

"Right." Randy was pleased to see Richard absorbing the ideas so well.

"What about two guys I saw who were after *one* rabbit; what were they doing wrong? They both believed they could find one, but only one rabbit showed up."

"I've seen it all before. This is how it usually goes: the men successfully imagined a rabbit, and they undoubtedly were excited about it. But when the one appeared, all application of proper thought went out the window. The competition ensued, and the one who finally caught it probably attributed it to his wit and never discovered true rabbit wealth. So long as he thought he had done it by his own clever strategy, he never found the power of working with God to provide all of his needs. On top of that, he probably lost his friend over the illusion that there was only so much to go around, and that one must be faster, quicker, and smarter than the next guy to win the prize."

"That would pretty much sum it up." Richard shook his head and chuckled as he thought, *Is there anything this man doesn't know?* Gathering his thoughts together, Richard asked, "So does this mean that we don't have to compete with anyone else to get what we want out of life?"

"That's the reality. There is more than enough for everybody, and to compete like that is actually in violation of another one of the laws of thought. That's the beautiful thing about it, Richard. God has provided enough for everyone who obeys these natural laws. If everyone believed and could visualize and truly expect to receive whatever they are asking of God, then everyone would receive. The laws of nature do not play favorites."

"I saw a couple of men competing for sacks on the path."

"Unnecessary. So long as they think there isn't enough to go around, they entertain a lie that prevents them from ever seeing what they are searching for."

"I was surprised to see the other men competing for a rabbit. I thought that to leave the path meant you were somehow on a higher plane or something like that and that you wouldn't operate that way."

Randy Mollup shook his head. "Oh, no. There are marvelously honorable men who never choose to leave the path which is entirely their prerogative. And then there are the blockheads who leave the path and do it all wrong. You'll find all kinds of people in both arenas. No, you don't have to leave the path to be happy. But isn't it nice to know you have options?"

"Yeah, it really is. Isn't that what freedom is all about? Having choices?"

"Having choices. Unfortunately, sometimes we learn too late that the choices we make have limited our ability to keep making choices. Eventually our poor choices lead to smothering bondage. That's how I felt right before I went on my very first rabbit hunt."

"What did you do? What was your first step away from the sack-race?"

"I imagined how it would feel to be free of it. Then I decided to find a way, somehow. Then I changed how I felt about the sacks...instead of grumbling about them, I started to appreciate them. Gratitude is a powerful thing. I think it put me in the right frame of mind to be able to see things I had never seen before. I started to see bigger and better sacks, and eventually I started seeing rabbits. When I was able to feel like they were already with me, the real magic began."

"Oh, wow." Randy's words distilled upon Richard's mind and he mused out loud, "I think I finally understand the gratitude part...I can go ahead and feel grateful that a rabbit is mine, because in my own mind, it *is*."

Randy was grinning, and nodding. "You got it. So, do you think you are ready to get your next rabbit?"

Richard panicked. Was Randy weaning him already? With his mind still in a spin, he suddenly had a hard time believing that any wild jackrabbit would actually be interested in going home with him, just because he felt grateful it was already his. "I'm not sure...what if a jackrabbit *doesn't* want to go home with me?"

"Look, I am going to tell you something profound, and I want you to remember this, and trust me: That which you want, is looking for you," Randy stated, and then emphasized again very slowly, "*That which you want... is looking for you.* In other words, you don't have to struggle to obtain it. Change your mental picture and expect that you will naturally attract all that you need."

"In other words?" Richard thought he was grasping it, but he wanted as much clarification as he could get. He didn't want this new way to become obscure...He wanted to *own* this information. He wanted to understand it well enough that it actually became a *part* of him.

"Well, changing your thinking literally changes *you*. You have been like a lantern with no flame, trying to...oh, I don't know," Randy grasped for a meaningful analogy. Finally he continued excitedly, "trying to gather an insect collection! Turn on your light, and they just come. Each person on the path is like a lantern that has burned out. It is a dream that can turn their light on, and then the bugs (or whatever they need to fulfill their dream), will be drawn to them, in a very natural way. Quite often, it isn't *circumstances* that need to change; it is the *person* that must change."

Change, Richard thought to himself. *Haven't I already changed? How much more do I have to change?* Changing oneself sounded harder than just chasing a rabbit. He thought back to Felicity's hurtful words, "Why can't you be more like your brother..." That cutting remark on top of everything else had moved him out of their door and into the forest. Couldn't he succeed just the way he was? Hadn't he already changed significantly? He *had* caught a rabbit, didn't that count for something?

It must have been the fallen look in Richard's face that led the good man to encouragingly clap his hand briefly on Richard's bicep. "Hey, it's not as hard as it might sound. Don't you see, when you allow the feelings I am talking about to grow within you, *that in itself* is facilitating the necessary change. That's it."

Richard felt encouraged so he didn't interrupt his teacher.

130

"Let's test it. How would you like to try it with something small, before going off to capture your next rabbit?"

"Yeah! Let's do that! If I could see this work in a small way, then I know it would help my confidence with the big dreams."

Randy spotted a monarch butterfly flitting about, not very far from them. Richard watched him close his eyes for a moment, and smile. He opened his eyes and stood up slowly, then approached the patch of blossoming clover where ten to fifteen more butterflies danced. But before getting too close to them, he sat down again and held out his finger, near a cluster of dainty white clover blossoms. In a minute or two, he slowly lifted his arm to show a butterfly comfortably perched on his finger.

Richard was amazed; Randy made it look so easy. Standing and then approaching the man, Richard said, "I don't think I could do that!"

"Then you can't, Richard. Pay attention to your thoughts. You have to allow yourself to believe in the impossible!"

Richard raised one eyebrow, and bit his lip.

"I have an idea. How do you feel about ants?"

"Ants? Now there's one thing I can believe will come to me. I am a magnet to the little buggers, they love to bite me, and I happen to be allergic."

"Perfect. Let's go find some ants."

"But that's not requiring that I believe in the impossible; that is asking that I simply believe in the inevitable!"

"Oh, no, Richard. This is all about getting whatever it is you want. Do you know what you want?"

"I *don't* want to get bit!"

"Then let's go find a massive colony of ants!"

I'll get what I ask for out of life...
I'll have the courage to ask.

I'll visualize the outcome, and the right people
will do the right things to help it happen.

There is more than enough for everybody.

~ CHAPTER FOURTEEN ~
THE REGRESSION

Richard puffed his cheeks and exhaled forcefully. "I thought this mental stuff was all about *attracting* what you want, not repelling what you don't want." Richard's trepidation about subjecting himself to a swarm of ants was unsettling.

"You're right. It is completely, one hundred percent about attraction. In your case, you will be attracting a healthy state of being, a condition of peace and contentment amid a colony of little red insects."

Randy grabbed Richard's shirt sleeve and pulled him over to a small clearing. Richard's heart began to race and his palms became sticky.

"Here are some. Now Richard, just do exactly what I say. I know you can do this."

Rubbing his hands on his pants, Richard took a deep breath and said, "Okay, I hope you're right."

Observing his moist hands, Randy asked, "What's wrong?"

"All I can see in my head is my poor hand all swollen and pocked with little red ant bites."

"Oh boy. This will be a challenge. Richard, do you think you could try to imagine your hand completely well, and safe, instead?"

"That's what I have to do, isn't it?"

"Yeah, it is."

"I'll try." With that, Richard closed his eyes, feeling somewhat silly, but not wanting to disappoint his mentor. He visualized his hand, just as it truly was, and breathed deeply until he had convinced himself that his hand was completely well and fine. Without opening his eyes, he told Randy, "I think I'm ready."

"Then come sit down and gently place your hand on the ground over here. If you start to panic, close your eyes again, and *PICTURE IT* again. Believe in the reality of the images of your mind. The truth is: your hand *is* well. If you believe that truth, it will continue to be reflected in your circumstances, for that is the circumstance with which you are in harmony. Remember the proverb, *as a man thinketh in his heart, so is he.*"

Richard sat down and placed his hand on the ground near the ants. It was a continual act of the will to keep discarding the fearful thoughts that nagged at him. He had never exerted so much energy to discipline his thoughts before. But he held firm to the image in his mind.

Finally Randy spoke. "Richard, they aren't bothering you. Do you see that? You did it."

136

Richard wasn't all that impressed, even though he was plenty grateful that he suffered no bites. Probably because he wasn't entirely sure it wasn't just a coincidence.

Randy detected his thoughts, and said, "It's okay to believe. It'll only strengthen your ability to have faith, and that's not a bad thing..."

Richard nodded, "Okay. I'll try to believe."

"Would you like to try it with something bigger before venturing back to the quest for rabbits? We could try for birds..."

"No thanks. I'd have to visualize my shirt remaining clean and fresh to avoid what the birds usually do to me. I'd like to just get on with the rabbit hunt, if you don't mind."

"That's fine, so long as you understand that if you put mental energy into images of things that you *don't* want, you will be counter-productive. You'll *attract* things you don't want..."

Richard couldn't quite put his finger on exactly why he was feeling this way, but he sensed that he was going into overload. Maybe it was just too much information too soon. His eyes scanned Randy's face, so animated, so enthused to share.

What was that on his nose? A hair? Richard was stunned. It was a really long hair. It must've been almost an inch long, coming out of the crease on the side of his nostril and curling slightly toward his cheek. How in the world had he missed it before? Distracted, Richard found it much easier to think of that hair than to think of what the man was saying.

Randy Mollup was still talking, and yet there was that hair. Richard couldn't stand it. He imagined plucking it out so he could finally concentrate again. He thought, *No, I couldn't do that. It would be a very bad thing to reach out and grab hold of that hideous hair. I can't let myself lift my hand, grip the hair and pull hard...I'd guess it would be pretty tough to yank. Huh,* he chuckled to himself, *I can nearly feel the brief resistance, and the almost audible 'doink' I'd feel in my fingers if I were to actually pull it out. No, I could never do such a thing...*

Without purposely replacing the thoughts in his mind, Richard eventually could even see Randy's face as though there were no hair. The thought was relieving, actually, and he felt like he just might be able to pay full attention again. With the distraction gone in his mind, he no longer felt irritated!

The smile spread across his face and Richard heard Randy continue, "...you'll find that your actions and your circumstances are nothing more than a reflection of the images in your subconscious mind."

Richard nodded. But before he knew it, his hand went up, and he actually reached out and snatched the hair right off of Randy's nose.

"What th–?" Surprised and shocked, Randy rubbed the side of his nose.

Richard's eyes were wide and he was mortified at what he had just done!

Gratefully, Randy only snickered. His snicker turned into a chortle and finally into an infectious belly laugh. He knew exactly what Richard had done: he had allowed a distraction to steer his thoughts. "A hair on my nose? You are distracted by a hair?! My friend, resolved thought takes practice." Randy pointed to Richard's rabbit, "And with a hare in your grasp and one less hair on my nose, you're on your way!" His eyes sparkled with humor.

Embarrassed, Richard laughed; then apologizing, he urged his mentor to continue. After all, the hair was gone, so it would be easier to pay attention, anyway. "I'm sorry. I'm afraid I allowed my thoughts to wander too long."

"That's okay. I think you have what you need to take it from here." He chuckled again and said, "Richard, it's no secret that the laws of thought played a predictable part in your behavior. You used the principles unknowingly to annihilate my nose hair. I suggest you pay close attention to your thoughts, for they *will* bear fruit. No action ever

139

occurs without first a thought of the same kind. So always choose those thoughts of yours carefully." Randy warmly whacked Richard in the leg with the back of his hand.

Richard was grateful that Randy seemed to be self-assured enough to gracefully handle the awkward moments they had experienced together.

Nobody spoke for a few minutes, yet the silence was anything but uncomfortable for either man. The mentor leaned back and watched the clouds travel by, and Richard remained thoughtful. He analyzed what had just happened with the hair incident. He realized that he truly *had* applied the laws of thought unconsciously, as he had almost automatically moved into action to remove the hair. He had done something completely out of character, without hesitation, and as a result, his immediate environment perfectly mirrored his thoughts. In his mind he had seen his instructor with a bald nose, and he had entertained some pretty strong feelings about it. As a result, he had moved automatically, almost unconsciously, into action to make it happen.

Undisciplined or improper thoughts could certainly get a man into trouble, Richard concluded.

The wind picked up some speed and the clouds rushed by. Richard wasn't sure how much time he had left with the good, round-bellied man, so he finally asked, "Let's say I do precisely what you are teaching me. How long could it take for my next rabbit to appear?"

"That depends on how long it takes for you to allow the changes inside of you to take place."

"So thinking and feeling will change me, eventually, huh." Richard still wanted to have a time frame on which he could rely.

"I know this part can be frustrating, the waiting part. But you have to understand, your lantern has to burn bright with the dream, and you must believe strongly. Sometimes it takes only a moment to truly believe something that you can't see; sometimes it takes months or years to develop that kind of expectation."

Months? Years? Richard fought the doubt that was creeping in. Richard wasn't a lazy man. He could work as many hours as anyone...but this was asking something else. The rabbit wriggled in his grasp, and Richard snapped his attention back to their conversation.

Randy sensed Richard may not be ready for all he wanted to say. But when Richard suddenly became alert, he continued. "Richard, for everyone who is committed to believing, no matter how long it takes...our dream eventually comes true. Isn't that a better guarantee than none at all? People who keep at it, trying to live in harmony with the laws of thought, will grow in skill and self-belief, until their confidence in getting everything they will ever need is virtually unshakable."

Forcing a smile, Richard reluctantly accepted that he would just have to take Randy's word for it at this point. Patience was something he would have to work on, and he knew it. "So you believe until it happens, and it doesn't matter how long it takes? Isn't it harder to believe, the longer you have to wait?"

"Now, remember, these principles can be used in small things that *don't* take a long time, all along the way. Such an exercise strengthens your will, and deepens your faith. Shoot, you could even use the principles to get better sandwiches in nicer bags if that was your dream. If you do, nature will create a need in one of the rabbit chasers who provide all these sacks; and they will feel compelled to leave just the right one for you to discover. As for the tougher dreams, you're right. It *can* be harder the longer you have to wait. But on the other hand, the longer you must wait, the more detail you can be putting into the image and the more certain you can become of precisely what you want."

"That sounds like a scapegoat to me, to be completely honest. Like, if it *never* happens, are we just supposed to say, 'oh well, I guess it's *still* on its way...forever'?"

"No, Richard. You can trust that each and every idea has an absolutely finite 'gestation period,' if you will. That period of time is specific and certain. Your job is to hang on to the belief throughout the required period of time. Pass the test, or should I say, the trial of your faith, and the reward is yours. Trust me, it's easier to do, just knowing the period of time is certain and finite. And one day, you'll be the one to provide a few bags for the good people on the path."

"Wouldn't it be nice if we had some sort of chart, listing all of the kinds of ideas in the world with all of the corresponding gestation periods?"

"Man, that *would* be something, wouldn't it."

Quietly the men contemplated the philosophies they had been discussing. Finally Randy broke the silence, "Richard, you can choose to be skeptical about dreams that don't show up on time. You can choose to think that what I'm telling you is a crock and that somehow my advice about unfulfilled dreams is a scapegoat. It's your choice, Richard. But remember, while you're wasting energy doubting, someone else out there is spending the same amount of energy believing, and *achieving*, and it might as well be you."

Not completely satisfied, Richard nevertheless recognized that he needed to try to do away with his analysis paralysis if he wanted to be the achiever of his dreams.

"If you choose to believe, then you can always chase doubts with this one thing: The times when we don't get what we want, exactly when we want it, we simply express gratitude to God for his wisdom and get excited because it means something better is on its way, or it wasn't what we would have wanted after all, or that it wasn't yet the right time. It's all good, and just thinking so will attract as much good to yourself and your family as you are capable of enjoying."

Richard conjectured, "So what if I get stuck just living my whole life with unfulfilled expectations?"

Sighing patiently, Randy thought for a moment then shared an analogy that he thought might be helpful now. "A woman expecting a baby knows that the baby will come. She doesn't have to know exactly when it will arrive, but she has a general idea, and she does not have to worry that she will live out her entire life with *that* unfulfilled expectation. Like I said, each of *our* dreams has a *finite* gestation period, Richard. Do not entertain doubts or fears, and you can be certain your dream will happen in the right time. Just as the woman doesn't want her baby to come too soon, neither should you want your dream to be realized too soon, either. When it doesn't seem to come on schedule, we must feel gratitude that it *will* come at the *right* time."

"Okay. Okay. I can see it in that light. If a woman is going to have a baby, she can predict its

144

arrival give or take a few weeks. She'll calculate a specific due date, which she usually marks on her calendar. But you're right, it could come a little early; and she isn't going to get doubtful if she goes overdue...in fact she'll get more and more certain all of the time, won't she? She won't give up and quit preparing; she'll just keep getting herself more prepared with each passing day. After all, she's *expecting*!"

"Well said, Richard. Imagine feeling that way about your dreams and goals. *Expect* them. And imagine becoming MORE sure the longer you have to wait."

"Now *there's* a new way of thinking. I like that."

Finding examples in nature always seemed to help. Once each idea 'clicked,' Richard felt amazed at how familiar it all seemed, like the laws of thought had always been a part of him, but he had not been aware. Perhaps the ideas resonated deep within him because he, himself, was a part of God's natural world, too. "Thank you, my four rabbit friend. Thanks a million. I can't wait to use what you've taught me to get my next rabbit."

"My pleasure, really. I wish there were more like you, because there's so much joy in sharing what I've learned."

With that, the small, heavy man smiled and tipped his head to say goodbye.

I'm expecting!

*I want my objective to happen
at the right time.*

~ CHAPTER FIFTEEN ~
THE SUCCESS

Richard looked down at the rabbit in his hand that had long since relaxed and accepted its capture. The rabbit belonged to Richard, and it seemed to be okay with that.

Richard closed his eyes and tried to visualize a rabbit in his other hand. It wasn't hard; all he had to do was duplicate how it felt from one hand that really had one, into the other. He realized it was so much easier to imagine holding rabbits after having been successful in catching one. And he finally understood why people like his brother Victor never seemed to worry about having what they needed, even when appearances indicated otherwise. Victor had always seemed to attract more opportunities and money so easily, according to his needs and desires. Additionally, he realized Victor was *not* all-consumed with riches like he had once thought. The process of accumulating wealth had happened naturally as he simply continued in right thinking.

He pulled his mind back from wandering to thoughts about Victor, and again focused on the second rabbit. He pictured it white, with brownish gray down its back and very large feet, and he felt the muscles in the ears twitching in his fist. Did it want to get away? No. It was twitching with excitement, because it wanted to be just where it was. A smile spread over Richard's face and he felt a swelling sensation of gratitude fill his chest. His throat tightened and his eyes became misty. Oh how wonderful it was to have such an abundance! How amazed he was that God had blessed him with so much, and so quickly! *Thank you! Thank you for such a wonderful blessing as a second rabbit to take home to my family! We are so happy and grateful for the ability I have to be with them again, and feel peace and joy, and the time I have to play with my son! To dance with my wife! To enjoy the wonderful things that were created for the purpose of showing mankind how much God loves his children!*

Richard didn't want to open his eyes, but when he did, there was the rabbit.

It didn't surprise him, for he was already grateful for it, and he already knew what it would feel like to hold it in his other hand. It was as predictable as an image in a mirror, only the reflection of his thoughts had not appeared immediately, but with a slight delay. He realized: that's okay. He was learning that he could expect his circumstances to mirror his thoughts, and he would be able to hold on and believe until they all came true.

The rabbit in front of him, this situation, was in perfect harmony with Richard's mind, and so it came together effortlessly. This time he didn't lunge at the hare, all he needed to do was open his fingers, and place them gently around the beautiful creature's ears.

~ CHAPTER SIXTEEN ~
THE RESOLVE

Felicity and Matthew walked into the woods; it was nearly dark. Each time she felt herself fear, or slip into a brief panic, she closed her eyes and whispered to herself. "When I have a choice, I choose to believe." She imagined hugging Richard again, then holding his face and telling him how sorry she was for not believing in him. She imagined saying how grateful she was for all of his attempts to provide. She pictured herself letting him know that it didn't matter if nothing changed, she could be happy just the way things were; after all, they had a roof over their head and they had each other. That's all they really needed, anyway! If they ran out of food (something she had worried about but never really expected could happen), then they'd starve together. But at least they'd do it together.

Felicity and Matthew walked hand in hand, talking about how good it was going to feel to find him. This lifted Matthew's spirits considerably as well as Felicity's, and they began to quicken their pace and leap the logs and rocks playfully together. He was out to find his Daddy, as in a game of hide and seek! "Dad-dy! I'm gonna find you! You can't hide from me!" Matthew jumped off of a rock and let out a giggle.

Felicity smiled and followed Matthew through the pines.

~ CHAPTER SEVENTEEN ~
THE TASK

Richard kept on. He had two rabbits in hand, and a heart full of gratitude. *These should last us a while*, he thought. Then, looking down, he spoke out loud, "Oh my! A boy *and* a girl rabbit! God sure knows how to give good gifts!"

A woman and a man passed by holding hands. "Isn't that the truth?" They smiled and Richard saw that they each held a rabbit, and at least twenty more were following behind, freely!

"What—how—?" Richard was speechless.

"Oh, this is what happens when you get good at writing your goals down and also when the goals are unselfish. All these rabbits are for others who are in need and are unable provide for themselves. God has proved that He can trust us with abundance, because we keep giving a portion away! The more we give, the more we get!"

Richard smiled. Once again he had that warm, familiar feeling of being right at home with a new idea.

The woman continued, "We gave even when we didn't have much to share. But we just decided early on that we would commit to giving away a percentage of all we were blessed with."

"I've known people that give and give and give, but I have never seen this kind of *getting* in my life!"

"That's because giving is only one part of it. The other part is knowing exactly what *you* want and *writing it down as though it is already yours.* If you don't make the formal request, it's like God has to operate as though you are content enough just the way things are."

"I *have* to write it down?"

"Yes, and then you know the rest. I see you have been successful in your own right." The woman referred to the two rabbits in Richard's hands.

"You mean, visualizing and feeling?"

"Yes, that's it."

Richard was no longer so amazed because now he was surrounded on all sides with people who had discovered the same principles. It just seemed normal to think this way. It would take some time to completely understand the gestation period thing in practical application, but he was willing to figure that out along the way.

He had some uncertainties, but at least he knew his part. He had control of, or at least a growing control, of his own thoughts. After all, that's all he *could* control, anyway. The timing

154

didn't really matter; he would leave that in God's hands.

He planned to write down in detail, a description of his life as he wanted it, as though it had already happened, with some *future* date at the top like a journal entry. He would allow himself to feel gratitude as though it was already his. And then he would let go and let God do the rest. And when a doubtful thought would come into his mind, he'd discard it. When he sensed that he should do this or that, he would do it, because he would trust that it was the voice of inspiration, leading him to accomplish his goal.

Then what about reuniting with his wife and son? He had what he needed...when would he get to be with them? How long would the rest of this journey have to take?

He realized there was something he hadn't done. He looked around because he didn't *have* a pen and paper to commit his desire in writing; and out there in the wilderness there was no hope of finding them. In fact, even if he did have a pen and a paper, his hands were busy holding jackrabbits. *I can't write it down; I don't even have a pen and paper. Surely I wouldn't be expected to chop a tree down and manufacture a pencil and paper just to write my goal! Besides, I don't have the foggiest idea where to come up with graphite for the lead. Now, if there was a store anywhere in sight I might be able to do something, but there is nothing around. Now what?*

Richard was frustrated and somewhat discouraged. *This isn't going to work for me. I **don't** have what I need, and couldn't do it even if I did, because my hands are full. Besides, there's nowhere to put the rabbits down without them wandering off. I don't believe that they'd just stay by my side, at least not yet.*

Then he remembered what to do, because now he was thinking like a winner. He closed his eyes and imagined a pen and paper in his hands, generating a feeling of gratitude. With not a clue about how it would help, he did it anyway.

Someone tapped him on the shoulder, interrupting his meditation and said, "Excuse me, mind if I hold your rabbits for just a moment? I've really needed to know what it feels like to hold rabbits; see, I'm trying to catch a few myself."

Richard smiled and said, "Of course."

But the man's hands were full...he was holding tight to a notepad and a pen, for he had just written down a goal of his own.

Richard said, "May I hold your things for a moment so your hands are free to hold the rabbits?"

"Oh, sure!"

"Would you mind if I took one of your papers for myself and borrowed your pen?"

"I'd be pleased."

156

The men traded rabbits for paper and Richard remembered: *That which you desire, is looking for you.*

Richard wrote a future date at the top of the paper. Then under the date he wrote: "I am so happy and grateful now that Felicity and I are together. Matthew is here and we are joyful and full of amazement at God's goodness to us. We have two rabbits, and know how to get more as needed! We feel peace and happiness as we play. Matthew and I enjoy throwing the ball and learning how to play catch together. Felicity and I enjoy dancing together and Matthew feels happy and secure in knowing that his parents love each other. We enjoy sharing what we have learned with friends and family, and anyone else who is seeking the wisdom of the ages...the laws of thought."

The man saw that Richard was done with the pen, and so he held out the rabbits and said, "Thank you very much, Mister. This is really going to help me imagine what it will be like for *me* to catch *my* first rabbit."

"My pleasure, young man. Thank you for the paper."

With that, Richard tucked the paper into his back pocket, took the rabbits from the young man, and walked on with an assurance and *expectation* that he would very soon be reunited with his family. After all, he had finally done all that he had

2222222

22222222222222222

been told to do. Expecting it now was easier than he ever thought it would be.

I will write a detailed description of my life as I want it, as though it has already happened, with some FUTURE date at the top like a journal entry. I will allow myself to feel gratitude as though it is already mine.

That which I desire is looking for me.

~ CHAPTER EIGHTEEN ~
THE BEGINNING

"Richard!" Felicity followed Matthew and continued to call for her husband.

"Dad-dy! Daddy, daddy, daddy!" Matthew sang, "I'm gonna find you!" Matthew climbed up on a large boulder and turned his head. "There he is, Mommy! We did it! We found him!"

Felicity ran to catch up with Matthew and sure enough, she saw Richard resting under the tree and against the rock.

"Is he asleep, Mom? Is that why he couldn't hear us?"

"Yes, Matthew." Felicity was confident. They approached him and Felicity gently shook his shoulder. "Richard, honey, it's time to wake up..."

Richard mumbled in his sleep, "Oh, thanks, but I already found a paper..."

"Richard, it's Felicity..." Her eyes were moist.

Richard opened his eyes and blinked a few times. Out of the corner of his eye he thought he saw a wild rabbit thump on a snake, leaving it almost, but not completely, lifeless and then dash away. He looked at Felicity and then at Matthew and tears of joy came to his own eyes. "Oh honey, it's so good to see you."

Felicity held his face and spoke softly, "Richard, I'm so sorry about what happened and how I acted. I'm *grateful* for you, Richard, and if nothing were to ever change, I'll be happy enough to just be with you."

"Oh, Felicity, everything is going to be okay. I know for a *fact* that everything is going to be just fine. Do you realize we have all we need to live abundantly and share a lot!? We're gonna be wealthy!"

Felicity pulled back with a perplexed look in her eyes. "How on earth is *that* going to happen?"

"I have no idea, but I know where to start. Felicity, what we want, wants us!"

"You know, Rich, it's gonna take a miracle."

"Yeah? Well, Felicity, I happen to believe in miracles."

Only a moment later, an unknown gentleman on the other side of Richard's very own town paused mid-sentence and told his dinner companion,

"...I just had an amazing idea..."

162

~ POINTS TO PONDER ~

Here's a list of the main ideas and questions from *The Jackrabbit Factor* which you may think about or ask yourself often. Refer to them regularly, and *believe in your dreams.*

- **What do I want?**
  I will spend time deciding exactly what I want, and why. I will set aside all the reasons it may seem impossible, and all the reasons I think it may fail while I allow myself to imagine a wonderful new picture for my life.

- **The passionate thoughts will emanate from my mind like radio waves causing unseen things to happen on my behalf.**
  I will enjoy success in my mind. I will feel the victory now; and I will know that these constructive thoughts are my little soldiers sent out to fight my battles ahead of me. They are preparing the way.

- **There is no obstacle so great that there is not also a way prepared for me to succeed.**
  There's always a way. If I can see it in my mind, and if it does not violate anyone else's free

165

agency, then it is possible. I will not give up until I find the way.

- ***I have all I need to get started, and that's all that matters.***
  Like an acorn in the ground, I will act on my immediate surroundings. In time, my connections will lead me to obtain all I need to accomplish my grand design.

- ***I will write it down. I will 'submit' my goal to the Master Chef.***
  I will expect my results to come just as I 'ordered'; therefore, I will be careful to be completely specific in my description. The more specific the desire, the more amazed I will be when it comes; and as a result I will know that its realization was no coincidence. I am continually grateful to the Master for all I receive.

- ***Whatever I need to accomplish my goal will be drawn to me once I have planted the seed in my mind.***
  I know that all I need is on its way...therefore, it is so.

- ***Whatever my circumstances are, I can always choose my own thoughts.***

166

As I believe that there is only abundance, my eyes will be opened to see solutions and opportunities that would otherwise be hidden from my view. I expect to find that which I seek. It is my choice to maintain an expectant mindset, which actually lights the way. Without an expectation, the way remains hidden in the darkness.

- ***When I have a choice, I choose to believe.***
It does me no harm to believe. If I am wrong, I will cross that bridge when I come to it. In the meantime, I have nothing to lose by believing. I choose to believe. It is a choice.

- ***Doubt not, fear not! It just simply isn't good for me.***
*Doubt and fear are emotions that can put me in harmony with the very thing I fear. I will choose to dismiss fearful and doubtful thoughts because they are mental images of circumstances that may never happen. Why would I ever want to waste mental energy attracting something I **don't** want?*

- ***How badly do I want wisdom?***
I expect to make sacrifices for wisdom. I eagerly make the necessary sacrifice because I know it will be worth the price. Wisdom may be

167

one of the only things I will take with me when I pass on. An investment in my knowledge will pay great dividends.

- **I'll get what I ask for out of life...I'll have the courage to ask.**
  I have nothing to lose by asking. If I hear "no," then I am no worse off than before. If I hear "yes," then I'll celebrate, and learn to expect "yes" more frequently.

- **I'll visualize the outcome, and the right people will do the right things to help it happen.**
  It is not for me to know who the right people are. I do not manipulate people with my thoughts; I simply emanate the desires of my heart and move my feet. Others who can help me along the way are also helped by me to accomplish their goals as well.

- **There is more than enough for everybody.**
  If the supply ever ran dry, more would be created out of the formless substance in the same way it was created in the beginning. There is no need for competition. By operating on a creative plane rather than a competitive plane, my eyes will continue to see opportunities and

abundance. Only by my doubt and fear will I ever live in scarcity.

- **I'm expecting! I want my objective to happen at the right time.**
  Just as a baby in the womb needs time to develop, so does my new idea. I will be patient and allow it to grow at nature's pace. I want it to arrive fully formed, healthy and strong. If I must wait longer than expected, my anticipation will only increase and I will continue to prepare for its arrival.

- **I will write a detailed description of my life.**
  I will describe it just as I want it, as though it has already happened, with a future date at the top like a journal entry. I will allow myself to feel gratitude as though it is already mine. I will experience it now.

- **That which I desire is looking for me!**
  Nature is friendly to my plans. I only have to go halfway, because that which I desire meets me in the middle. I know that as I continue to move toward the accomplishment of my goal, the outcome is approaching me just as rapidly.

~ A FEW EXTRA ~
POINTS TO PONDER

From the Epilogue which follows

I will scrutinize each word in my goal, or gratitude statement.
I will write a future date at the top: a date I hope to see the dream come true. The date is far enough away to be believable, but close enough to keep me awake at night. I will only choose words for my gratitude statement which make me think of the positive aspects of the dream. I will write in present tense, and describe how it feels "now that I enjoy" the success. I will follow the format: "(Date): I am so happy and grateful now that I enjoy...Because..."

* *Goal first, way second.*
  I will not select the goal based on a way I already have in mind. If I do, then I am not dreaming big enough. I will select the goal based on the desires of my heart. The way will come **after** *the goal is properly set; after I have composed and internalized my gratitude statement.*

- *I know exactly what fear is, and it doesn't stop me.*
  If I feel fear or anxiety related to achieving my goal, I know it's simply my subconscious mind wrestling with two contradictory truths such as "I am broke" and "I am wealthy." Fear is evidence that I have successfully turned over the new idea to my subconscious mind through emotion; and if I persist in spite of the fear, I will overcome old programming. In the face of anxiety, I will proceed anyway.

~ EPILOGUE ~

Almost Twelve Years Later...

"So did you get the English project done for Ms. Bear?"

"Are you kidding? She'd have had my head if I didn't. I've got it right here, ready to go. What about you?"

Moaning, the young man replied, "Oh, I *wish*! Still have a couple things to do but plan on throwing it together at lunchtime."

"Oh, *Kyle*! You can't miss lunch! Matt's sixteen! Don't you wanna see what kind of wheels his rich daddy gave him? He'll probably take us off campus to get something from Lumpy's Lunch! Come *ON*!"

The young man who didn't finish his project was disappointed to miss out. "Oh, that *stinks*." Sighing, he said, "No, I need an 'A' on this one."

"Your loss. I bet it's a BMW. No, I bet it's a Lamborghini. Can you imagine the heads that'll turn when we go cruisin' with Matt? I bet Jenna would give you a second glance, you sure you can't turn in the project tomorrow?"

"There's no way, Josh. No can do."

"Your loss."

Just then a vibration rattled the ground and the young men felt it come up through their feet. With wide eyes, they looked at each other and then turned around to see an old beater truck coming their way and in obvious need of a muffler. In fact, as it jiggled side to side on its approach toward them, the boys could see that the dilapidated, gray and rust truck had been in a wreck, and one fender was barely held on with a wire wrap.

Heads *did* turn, including Jenna's. She was walking from her outdoor locker, headed toward the main building on the campus when she saw the jalopy rattle in to the parking lot and approach the boys who were leaning against an old Volkswagen. The truck pulled in right next to the VW and Matt kicked the door open from the inside and climbed out.

"Hi guys."

The boys were speechless. Kyle caught a glimpse of Jenna with a look of disgust on her face as she quickly turned away, hoping to avoid eye contact with them.

Matt took a deep breath and exhaled slowly. "Gotta go. Class is about to start." Matt slammed the door shut and began to head for the main building.

The two other boys looked at each other questioningly, and then jogged ahead to catch up with Matt.

174

EPILOGUE

"Matt—what's going on? What was THAT?!"

Matt didn't look at his friend. "What's what, Kyle?"

"The truck! Where'd it come from? Why'd you come to school in *that* thing?"

"That's my new car, Kyle. I *use* it to get to *school*. Have you got a problem with that?"

Josh piped in with a chuckle, "That's no *new car*, Matt."

"Yeah, Matt, where's the *wheels?*"

"What are you saying, Josh?"

Glancing at Kyle, Josh paused and then cautiously replied, "Matt, you're sixteen. You're dad's loaded. Where's the *car?* We expected something more along the lines of a BMW, or..."

"Lamborghini..." Kyle interjected.

Matt stopped abruptly and turned to face Kyle and Josh straight on. "Look, guys. My *dad's* rich. I'm not." With that he glanced up at the big round clock on the wall above the junior class bulletin board and said, "I've gotta go. Later, guys."

As Matt jogged ahead, disappearing into the crowds, the two boys shook their heads. "What's Jenna gonna think now?" Kyle whined.

"Forget it, Kyle. You just need to get your own wheels if you want to turn *her* head. If Matt *had* brought a new car, she probably would've fallen for him instead of you, anyway."

175

~~~~~

"Dad, I don't think I can take it. Everyone just glared at me today. There're kids whose folks are *out of work* that have nicer cars than me."

"Are you trying to out-do them? Do you think you deserve better than them?"

"No, it's not that, Dad. It's just that— it just isn't fair."

"When you can afford a nice car, you can get yourself a nice car. What's so unfair about that?"

"You always make things so difficult! Seems like everyone else is just *given* a car when they're sixteen: a car with *paint*."

Rich chuckled empathetically. "Son, one day you'll thank me. To be honest with you, I feel sorry for the kids who have everything just given to them. Mark my words; you'll have more going for you in the long run."

Matt growled and rolled his eyes. "You just don't *get* it." Storming away, Matt slammed the door behind him causing his father to wince. Rich simply shook his head, grinning, and then turned his chair around to get back to his paperwork.

~~~~~

One Week Later...

THUD! Matt slammed his books on the floor of the home office, causing his father to spin around, startled.

"Dad, I CAN'T take it anymore! Rachel turned me down for Saturday night, and I *know* it's because she's embarrassed about the truck!"

"Son, then she's not worth your time. Anyone who is *that* caught up in appearances has very little else going for them. You'll find a gal who likes you for who you are."

"I know, I know. You've ingrained that in me for as long as I've cared about girls. I *know* that, Dad. It's just hard when reality hits, and you find out that there *aren't* any girls out there like that."

"Do you really believe that, son?"

Matt sighed. He knew what his dad was getting at, and decided to save his father the trouble of pontificating 'lecture number six.' Tipping his head from side to side, he rehearsed it all: "No, dad. There's a girl who'll like me for who I am, and who has enough integrity to abide by universal principles of right living." It was a canned line that he had repeated over and over thanks to a stubborn father who wanted his son to find the most possible joy in life.

"Son, you really want a different car?"

Matt's posture fell and his eyes widened as if to convey the message: *"Isn't that obvious?!"*

"Matt, you don't want a different car. Deep down you're completely comfortable with the old truck."

"Dad! How can you say that?! I *hate* that truck!"

"On the surface you hate it, but it's in perfect harmony with your subconscious mind, Matt. If you want different wheels, you've gotta change what's in your subconscious mind."

Matt sighed. Sometimes his dad's lectures were downright unbearable.

Rich could read his thoughts. "Son, it doesn't matter to me what you drive. But when it matters to you so much that you're ready to learn, just let me know. We all pay a price for knowledge, your price is to gut it out and put up with a few lessons from your old man." With that, Matt's father tipped his head down and raised his eyebrows, and then swiveled his chair back around to face his desk.

Matt closed his eyes and shook his head. "Dad, I know I shouldn't want a new car just to impress the girls. Is it okay, though, to want one that isn't an *eyesore?* Just, I don't know, so that our community is a little nicer with one less junk heap on the road?" Matt tried to sound less like a teenager and more like a grownup. Deep down Matt didn't wish for a new car *primarily* to impress the girls; he just didn't want the car to repel them, either.

Without turning around, his father said, "So do you want a nicer car or not?"

"I want a nice car, Dad. But I don't have the money, and I know you aren't going to buy one (even though you can *afford* it)," Matt couldn't resist dropping the last line under his breath. Perhaps it would guilt his father into giving in.

Rich didn't reply at all.

Eventually the silence made Matthew feel awkward, and he wished he hadn't tried to manipulate his dad. He knew better. His father was extremely principled, which made it impossible to persuade him against his standards. Pushing his father only left Matt feeling uncomfortable.

Matt relaxed his posture and shook his head. "I'm sorry, Dad. Will you just tell me how you think I'm supposed to get myself a nice car when I can only work part-time at minimum wage?"

Turning in his chair, his father replied, "I have no idea. That's a question only you will be able to answer. I can't be the one to tell you where to jump, in order to catch your rabbit. Only you will know that, once you spot it. You're the only one who'll know which way the rabbit leads you."

The rabbit analogy was not a new one to Matt. He'd heard it all his life, but until now he never really felt the need to understand it.

After spending the better part of an hour rehearsing the analogy, and reviewing certain sections in Richard's book called, "The Jackrabbit Factor," Matt decided he'd better write his goal down.

"Once you get it on paper, bring it to me and I'll check to make sure you've worded it properly."

Matt disappeared to his room for five whole minutes. When he returned, he showed his father a statement which read, "I will have a nice car next week."

Rich looked at it and tried to hide his dissatisfaction, "Do you believe this is true?"

"No, but you've said before to write it down, even if it is unbelievable."

Quietly Rich mumbled, "This isn't quite right." Louder, he said, "Let me ask you something: If you already *had a way*, how long do you think it'd take to get the car?"

"If I had a way? Oh, I don't know. That depends on how good of a way it was."

"How *good of a way* it is depends on how good of a way it *needs to be* in order to reach the GOAL. *Goal first, way second.* Not the other way around. The way only shows up after you've set the goal. If you never set the goal, you have no need for the way."

"Then how do I decide on the *when?*"

"Well, when do you *want* the car?"

EPILOGUE

"Yesterday!" Matt was aggravated.

"Matt, since this is the first big rabbit you've ever tried to catch, I suggest you pick a date far enough out that it is relatively believable, but close enough that it keeps you awake at night."

"Oh, I don't know. Maybe three months?"

"That could be good...pick a day."

Matt paused, but finally moaned, "But I don't *want* to have to wait three months, Dad."

"Son, sometimes waiting can be excruciating. But once I've helped you set the goal properly, you'll be just as excited as the day it'll be yours, and nothing anyone can say will get to you. You'll be locked on the dream, and you'll enjoy the journey. When someone teases you about your truck, you'll have an inner confidence that won't be rattled, because you'll *know* that it's only a matter of time before you'll have your car. Trust me, when you're chasing a rabbit, you don't have time to hear what people on the path are saying about you."

Matt's defiant attitude had completely melted away, and he meekly listened to his father's counsel. Deep down, he truly respected his dad. His father was well thought of in the community and at church, and Matt was proud of that. Life at school among his peers was rough, though. It wasn't easy to disregard the taunting at school. Still, all he had to do was look at the kind of life enjoyed by his dad; then compare it with the lives of his friend's

181

parents. By doing so, he was smart enough to know from whom he should receive counsel.

"Now," his father continued, "go write the goal again, this time with a specific date at the top. And while you're at it, add some detail in a description of the car you want."

Later, Matt returned with, "April 14, [year]: I will have a new, shiny black convertible."

His father looked it over and said, "Good, that's a little more than three months from now. Only there's a problem."

"What's that?"

"According to this goal, in three months you'll still be driving your truck."

"What do you mean? It says I'll have a convertible."

"It says you 'will' have a convertible. That word insinuates that the convertible is still in your future. So in three months, you are no closer to having it than you are now."

"Oh, wow. I never thought of that."

"Write it in present tense, as though it's already yours, and express how it feels to have it. And, it could use a little more detail, too."

"Why?"

"Because a *vacuum cleaner* can be convertible. Exercise equipment can be convertible. If you don't want a vacuum cleaner, you'd better be specific. Son, I knew a lady once who set a goal to have ten thousand dollars in her hand by a certain date. She had long since put the idea out of her mind, but when the day came, she found herself at the bank filling out a deposit slip for her father's bank account. The date triggered her memory of the goal she had written much earlier, and so she slowly turned the check over to find that the amount was exactly ten thousand dollars. She got exactly what she had asked for: ten thousand dollars in her hand on that date, but the problem was that the money didn't belong to her; she was making a deposit for her father. She hadn't been specific enough when she committed her goal to paper."

"Is that a true story?"

"That story is absolutely true. The woman's name is Camille."

"Why do we *have* to be so specific? If what we want comes to us from the Universe somehow, isn't God smart enough to know what we want, and get it right without all the fuss of us writing it down perfectly?"

"Of course He already knows what we want, but we're told to ask for it. I believe that we often get what we ask for, even if it isn't what we meant, simply to teach us a lesson about how much control we really have over the kind of life we live. How specific we want to be is entirely up to us."

"What if I say it this way: 'April 14, [year]: I now have a shiny black convertible Mustang and it feels great.'"

"That's closer. But it needs more description, more *feeling.*"

"You sound like Ms. Bear now, my English teacher."

"Come on, make it real."

"Um…how about, 'April 14, [year]: I am so excited now that I have a shiny black convertible Mustang that is less than five years old. It is so much fun to go cruising with my friends, and I don't have to be embarrassed about it looking hideous."

"Okay, that's better, but since our subconscious mind takes entire sentences and registers each word rather than complete phrases, that goal would program your subconscious mind to help you find a hideous and embarrassing shiny black convertible Mustang that is five years old."

Matt sighed. His dad was being just like Ms. Bear: so picky, and hard to please.

"Son, to help you understand this, let's talk about people that try to 'lose weight.' So long as they are focused on 'losing weight,' they are setting themselves up for failure. Why? Because when our subconscious mind hears that we've 'lost' something, it automatically kicks into gear in an effort to help us 'find' what we have lost. When it hears the word 'weight,' it automatically associates the term with synonyms such as 'heaviness' or 'paper weight,' or 'weights and measures.' So to set a goal to 'lose weight,' a person is actually programming their subconscious mind to 'find heaviness'!"

"So what should they do instead?"

"They should write a date, and then express how grateful they are now that they enjoy a healthy, energetic, slender body."

"Hmmm. Nice!"

"And they should spend more time looking at slim pictures of themselves than they do looking at themselves in the mirror. Doing so will help their subconscious mind eventually be in harmony with the results they seek, and the results will come more naturally, and more permanently. Looking in the mirror all the time and checking the scale every day only reinforces the heavy image they are trying to overcome. It wouldn't do any harm to manipulate the display on the scale to show the number they *want*. Doing so could actually help their subconscious mind believe it's true, and automatically help them desire the proper diet, or lead them to the right so-called 'weight loss' program."

"Makes sense, I guess."

"Same thing goes for getting out of debt. People need to quit setting goals for 'getting out of debt' because they're programming their mind to focus on *debt*. Doing so will only attract a constant supply of debt into their life. Not only that, but they'd be training their subconscious mind to constantly *pay down* debts. Do you know what that means? When their bills are finally paid off, their subconscious mind will panic. No debts to pay, but a well-established order to pay off debts. To solve this problem, it will automatically lead the person to create more debt."

Matt's mind was drifting, since dealing with debts wasn't something with which he was personally familiar. His father nevertheless continued, as if lost in the memory of previous conversations he had with people who often sought his advice.

"Instead, a debt-ridden person needs to create a gratitude statement like, 'I am so happy and grateful that I keep my financial promises on time, and that I am independently wealthy. It feels absolutely empowering now that I hold the title to my car and the deed to my home! I feel so free now that my bank account always has at least X amount of money in it.'" Rich paused. He was obviously contemplative, as if attempting to fine-tune his philosophy on the matter.

Politely Matt humored his father and said, "Remind me about all that when it's news I can use, Dad."

Snapping back to the issue at hand, Rich obliged, "You, Matt...you're subconsciously in harmony with the old truck. If you want to own a nice car, you have to switch the self-image you have deep inside your subconscious mind. You do that by writing your goal properly, and reading it often enough that you can actually feel how it'll be when it's yours. See, our subconscious mind accepts anything it receives as truth. Then it kicks things into gear to make sure that *what it believes to be true* becomes or remains our reality. Emotion actually reinforces subconscious ideas. The fact is, that every day you feel emotionally upset about having an ugly truck, your subconscious mind is solidified with the truth that you own an ugly truck."

"My *truth* is that I own an ugly truck? Because I let myself feel emotional about it?"

"That's right. If you want to change your *truth,* you must have a stronger emotion about a replacement idea such as, 'I feel absolutely ecstatic that I now own a nice, shiny Mustang,' and so forth. If you can genuinely feel how you *expect* to feel, you are essentially handing your subconscious mind a *new* truth. On a conscious level, you might feel like you're lying to yourself, but do it enough and you will literally drown out the old, undesirable programming. You will put yourself in tune with the new circumstance you desire, and all that you need in order to see it through will be drawn to you."

"So how do I write the goal properly, then?" Matt was fascinated by the whole idea.

His father replied, "Let's say you wrote a goal like, 'April 14, [year]: I am so happy and grateful now that I own a [model year] shiny black convertible Mustang with low miles. I am grateful that it runs properly and gets me where I need to go. It is so much fun to cruise around with the blue sky overhead. I am grateful that it is a dependable way to get me to school and my other responsibilities. I am amazed at the worthy money-making opportunity which presented itself to help me get this car. The Mustang was affordable and leaves me free financially to pursue other goals such as college. I am grateful that I had plenty of time for the money-making idea which presented itself and allowed me time to pay sufficient attention to my studies to keep my grades up. The kids at school are inspired by the example I have set, and are curious to know what Dad has taught me. I selflessly share what I have learned and encourage others to set worthwhile goals. I attract the kinds of friends who respect me for my integrity; after all, I only wanted the car for respectable reasons.'"

"Wow, Dad. That was a mouthful. Are you serious?"

Rich just smiled. "Son, it's all up to you. You set a goal like that, and read it often, and eventually you will honestly begin to believe it's all true. Once you are already living the dream in your mind, it's only a matter of time before it's really yours. You'll be in tune to opportunities that come your way which will assist you in attaining your goal."

Matt was intrigued. He believed what his father was saying, because his father had obviously practiced his theory successfully for years, and soon Matthew's mind was racing with anticipation. Abruptly he declared, "I'll be in my room Dad, thanks!"

He ran upstairs and pulled out a page from his notebook. Carefully and thoughtfully he composed a statement which described how he felt about his car, and life in general, or how he expected it to be, three months in the future. After about two hours, he returned to his father's office but his father wasn't there. "Dad? Where are you?!"

"I'm in the kitchen with your mother!" His father called from another room.

Matthew ran to the kitchen and slid to a stop on the polished floor, nearly falling over but catching himself by grasping onto the granite countertop. "Dad, I think I've got it! Look at this!"

Rich read the statement. It was nearly a whole page long, and it was obvious that Matt had scrutinized each word. "You know how I can tell you've planted this dream seed properly, Son?"

Felicity had just poured three tall glasses of iced lemonade and beamed with pride.

"How, Dad?"

"Because you're genuinely excited about your new car. Look at him, Honey. He can hardly stand still."

Matthew *was* jittery. He couldn't wait to *do something* about finding a way now. "Dad, that's my car! I am getting a new car."

"I know, Son. How are you going to do it?"

"I don't know yet, but somewhere that car sits, just waiting for me to find it. And somewhere, there are people who need me to do something for them, and they'll give me the money I need. I just *know it,* Dad. I'm going for a ride. We'll see where it leads me."

"Take my phone in case we need to find you, dear." Felicity reached into her purse and handed Matthew the tiny device.

"Son, don't be discouraged if you don't find something right away..."

"Oh, Dad. I already know that. This trip today might only lead me to think of something else I should do instead tomorrow. It's all good...that's what you've always taught me."

"And Son, if you feel fear or anxiety right before you act on a hunch related to achieving your goal, just know that it's simply your subconscious mind wrestling with two contradictory truths. It is trying to believe 'my car is an ugly truck' and 'my car is a shiny black Mustang' all at the same time. The anxiety is only a sign that your new image has found its way solidly into your subconscious mind. It's simply a positive sign that you've done it. You've successfully planted the new idea in your subconscious, so take action anyway!"

Matt stopped just before disappearing out the door and said, "Huh?" He couldn't seem to concentrate on what his father just said; his mind was already miles down the road.

"Oh, never mind. We'll have that conversation soon enough I'm sure."

"Okay, Dad!" With that, he was gone. His parents smiled and gave each other a squeeze. This experience alone was worth all the agony of refusing to give him the world on a silver platter. Felicity confessed, "I was wrong, Rich. I shouldn't have given you so much grief over what to do for his birthday."

"Oh, I can't blame you. It's so hard to do the right thing. Sometimes you're the one that sets *me* straight. I'm just grateful that we endured the hard times together and can now help each other remember to try to live according to principles."

~~~~~~

"Hey guys, let's go off campus for lunch today. I'd like to swing by the used car lot down on the corner," Matt said as he approached his buddies near the lockers.

"What, and take your truck? Thanks, but no thanks. Besides, I heard Jenna's sticking around at lunchtime to work on some posters for student council," Kyle glanced over his shoulder in case he could spot her across the way.

Josh jumped in, "Matt, I can't believe you'd want to drive your truck at *lunchtime* when all the other cars from school are out on the road. Save it for the 'to and from,' my friend."

"Look, who *cares* what I'm driving?" Matt's demeanor was solid. "I'm going to take my truck at lunch, and I am going to the used car lot. I saw a black convertible Mustang there on my way to school, and I've gotta see if it's mine. I have to check the year, and the mileage, and if it's the one, find out how much money I have to make in order to get it. I'm gonna sit in it if they'll let me, and I'm gonna see how it feels."

"You're a goofball, Matt," Kyle chuckled.

"See you after lunch, guys." Matt turned, threw his backpack over his shoulder, and was gone.

"Hey Matt! You think you'll get a Mustang? In your dreams!" Josh hollered and laughed out loud.

Matt didn't turn around. He just grinned and thought, *That's precisely why it's **gonna** happen: because it **is** in my dreams...*

Walking to his truck, he heard Kyle say, "Oh, he's just excited, Josh. Give him a week."

Matt glanced back at the guys who were on their way to the cafeteria. He wondered why they had to try to pull him down like that. *I guess I need to add something to my goal about the kinds of friends I spend my time with.*

His trip to the lot occupied his entire lunch period. He even forgot about and never missed the lunch he brought from home...*a peanut butter sandwich in a brown paper sack*...after all, he was simply too busy chasing his rabbit.

~ ABOUT THE AUTHOR ~

Leslie Householder is a wife and mother of seven children. She is the founder of ThoughtsAlive.com, ProsperTheFamily.com and the author of "Hidden Treasures: Heaven's Astonishing Help with Your Money Matters."

While she has been a seminar speaker and personal success coach since 2002, the age and stage of her young family has been her motivation to compose a message which will continue to reach her audience even while she spends time with her preschoolers and changes diapers at home (approximately 37,755 diapers so far and still counting).

She's been a guest speaker at numerous venues with classes which she has authored including, "Working with your Subconscious Mind to Achieve your Goals," "Leaning on the Lord in a Financial Crisis," and "Tuning in to the Abundance God has for You." She has held numerous teleclasses servicing participants across the world, and also conducted live seminars as a facilitator for Bob Proctor's Life Success programs in several states in the continental U.S. She is a contributing author to the "Chicken Soup for the Soul" series, and her articles have circulated in internet ezines and print magazines alike.

You can learn more about Leslie and her message at ThoughtsAlive.com. Sign up for her ThoughtsAlive Newsletter and/or her Insight of the Day to encourage you and strengthen your resolve to reach your highest potential.

~ RECOMMENDED RESOURCES ~

(Before considering any recommended resource, be
sure to decide what, specifically, it is that you
want. You'll only be drawn to the right path after
you've spotted your 'rabbit'. Remember, it isn't the
program that will be responsible for your success, it
is the inner voice which directs you to the right
program, *after* you've identified your goal.)

What is one goal you already have in mind?

Target Date: _____

"I am so happy and grateful now that

_____

_____

_____

_____

_____

_____

_____

_____

_____

_____

_____
                                             "

After you've "picked your picnic" (as described in the preface) you may want to check out some of these recommended resources to see if any of them seem like the right thing for you to do next.

Insight of the Day

An inspirational thought each Monday through Thursday, and a heartwarming story each Friday, delivered to your email box. This is a great way to keep your thoughts where they need to be on a daily basis. Also gives you access to special offers from some of the greatest leaders in the self-help industry.

Available at www.thoughtsalive.com

Jackrabbit Factor Flash Movie

A brief (four-minute) flash movie based on the book. Watch it to remind yourself of one of the most prominent ideas from the story. Use it to share what you've learned with your friends, family, and associates. Use the movie in work presentations or training meetings. This movie emphasizes the importance of goal setting, and following one's own rabbit instead of jumping and barking at air.

www.jackrabbitfactor.com

RECOMMENDED RESOURCES

Jackrabbit Factor Book on Audio
Pop it in your car on family trips for your children to enjoy, or listen to it while you're commuting to help keep your head in the game on a regular basis. *Available at www.thoughtsalive.com.*

Hidden Treasures: Heaven's Astonishing Help with Your Money Matters
Paperback book. This is Leslie's personal spiritual perspective on the seven laws of thought mentioned so often in The Jackrabbit Factor. "If the righteous shall prosper, why am I so broke?" Learn the laws; conscious awareness of them alone is enough to help eradicate fear and uncertainty about your future. (Though quoting a number of different religious sources, the fundamental ideas presented do not exclusively represent the beliefs or doctrines of any specific denomination. The principles are universal. It's all about having faith, and what Leslie personally thinks are the nuts and bolts of what it is that makes faith work.) *Available at www.thoughtsalive.com*

Jackrabbit Factor PDF eBook and follow-up eLessons

The Jackrabbit Factor book in PDF format available for immediate download with refresher lessons and reminders delivered to your email box.

Available at www.thoughtsalive.com

Hidden Treasures: Heaven's Astonishing Help with your Money Matters PDF eBook and eLessons

An in-depth look at the seven laws of success from Leslie's personal, spiritual perspective. Is it right or wrong to seek riches? "If the righteous shall prosper, why am I so broke?" "Am I violating any of the laws on a consistent basis, without even realizing it? Am I unknowingly saying 'No thank you' to God when He tries to send a blessing my way?" We're governed by the laws each moment of each day. Blessings flow abundantly to those who obey these seven laws. Content is the same as the Hidden Treasures paperback book, but this is available as an immediate download, and has optional follow-up lessons delivered to your email box to help you stay on track. You'll feel the support extend beyond your initial purchase. (Although the book quotes material drawn from various religious literature, the ideas presented do not exclusively represent the beliefs or doctrines of any specific denomination. The principles are universal. It's all about faith, and what Leslie personally thinks are the nuts and bolts of what it is that makes faith work.)

Available at www.thoughtsalive.com

RECOMMENDED RESOURCES

Other resources available at Thoughtsalive.com

Customize the resource pages for YOUR organization!

Use this book as a powerful contacting tool. Share it with your prospects and BE the mentor they turn to when they're finished reading it! Imagine YOUR contact info printed in the pages at the end of the book!

Use the book as a primer for new sales team members, distributors, management, leadership...

Promote YOUR services as the recommended resources!

Visit ThoughtsAlive.com to check on current availability and terms of this "Customize the Book" service.

Contact the author by visiting THOUGHTSALIVE.COM
or send comments and bulk rate requests to

Leslie Householder
THOUGHTSALIVE BOOKS
P.O. Box 31749, Mesa, AZ 85275

Printed in the United States
74426LV00001B/130-999